MONEY-MAKING
CANDLESTICK
PATTERNS

Backtested for Proven Results

STEVE PALMQUIST

Marketplace Books
Columbia, Maryland

Publisher: Chris Myers

VP/General Manager: John Boyer

Development Editor: Jody Costa

Art Director: Larry Strauss

Cover Design: Jennifer Marin

Interior Design & Production: Jennifer Marin

Production Coordinator: Chris Franks

This publication is designed to provide accurate and authoritative information in regard to the subject matter covered. It is sold with the understanding that neither the author nor the publisher is engaged in rendering legal, accounting, or other professional service. If legal advice or other expert assistance is required, the services of a competent professional person should be sought.

From a Declaration of Principles jointly adopted by a Committee of the American Bar Association and a Committee of Publishers.

Library of Congress Cataloging-in-Publication Data

Palmquist, Steve.
  Money-making candlestick patterns : backtested for proven results / by Steve Palmquist.
     p. cm.
  ISBN-13: 978-1-59280-328-6 (hardcover)
  ISBN-10: 1-59280-328-8 (hardcover)
  1. Stocks--Charts, diagrams, etc. 2. Stocks--Prices--Charts, diagrams, etc. 3. Stock price forecasting.
  4. Investment analysis. I. Title.
  HG4638.P35 2008
  332.63'2042--dc22

                             2007052107

Printed in the United States of America.

TERMS OF USE & DISCLAIMER

ACKNOWLEDGEMENTS

This book provides an opportunity to share some of my research in trading techniques. It would not have been possible without others who came before me. Thanks to those who uncovered and published candlestick patterns. Thanks to those who developed backtesting and charting software that allows average traders to effectively test and use trading patterns. Many people have contributed to the tools that have allowed me to conduct and share this research. I hope this book is another link in the long chain of trading tools and techniques that provide an edge to active traders.

I would like to thank my wife, Mary, who has encouraged me to share my research. You have always been there for me. You are my sunshine.

Thanks to Charles, who got me interested in technical analysis, and Kevin, who provided a weekly forum for discussing trading.

Thanks to the subscribers of my newsletter, *The Timely Trades Letter*. Some of your questions have led to interesting areas of research, which I will continue to share in the *Letter*.

TABLE OF CONTENTS

-PREFACE-

Money-Making Candlestick Patterns is written for active traders interested in results and specific ways to improve their trading. During 20 years of active trading experience, I have researched, tested, and analyzed a number of trading systems and techniques. Some have shown promising results, others have not. That's because each trading technique, including candlestick patterns, has market conditions during which it works best. One way to determine when to use a tool—and when to avoid it—is to analyze the tool's performance through backtesting. Backtesting, which shows how a trading pattern has worked over time, is not a guarantee of future performance. But, it certainly makes more sense to use a tool that has performed well in the past than one that hasn't.

Making money in the stock market requires knowledge of what to trade, when to trade, and how to use trading tools designed for different market conditions. Just as a carpenter will use different tools when building a house, traders will use different tools to build their accounts. Using the same trading tool in all situations is like trying to build a house with just a hammer.

Carpenters have tools designed for specific jobs, and so should traders. Candlestick patterns can be effective trading tools, and the wide variety of candlestick patterns allows traders to select the ones most appropriate for the current market environment.

But, the trader, like the carpenter, must go beyond just acquiring the tools. Traders must understand which tool to use for each specific task and have a clear understanding of how the tool works—what can and cannot be done with it. This book shares insights and research into what does and does not work when trading candlestick patterns. After reading this book, you will know which patterns are most effective in which markets, and how different parameters or filters may change results.

Some tools, like a screwdriver, are fairly easy to learn how to use. Other tools, like a table saw, require more training and experience to get the most out of it. Most carpenters serve an apprentice period during which they work with and learn from someone with years of experience. It is amazing how many people will just start trading their hard-earned money without first "learning the trade." Understanding how to trade candlestick patterns requires the ability to recognize the basic pattern and, also, knowledge of the market environments in which they work best.

I add tools to my trading toolbox based on their effectiveness. Trading systems are not effective because someone told you about them; they are effective because they work. In this book, I've done the heavy lifting for you. Candlestick patterns, like most trading systems, are affected by market conditions, volume patterns, and other factors. This book will not only teach you how these parameters influence trading results, but also will give you the specific results so you know when to trade a particular pattern and when to use another tool in your toolbox.

The first chapter of this book outlines candlestick basics, including their background, how to recognize different candlestick patterns, definitional issues, and several issues and requirements related to testing the effectiveness of candlesticks. The subsequent chapters provide more information on individual patterns, how variations in the parameters of their definitions affect performance, and how the trading patterns perform in different market environments. I will finish the book with a chapter on my particular trading strategy and how you can put these results to work right away.

But trading is more than just understanding the effectiveness of different trading patterns. There are no perfect trading systems, no matter what those slick brochures may say. Trading is a statistical business in which it is important to manage risk. Every trading system has a certain percentage of winners and losers. If you bet big, or leverage the account with margin or options, you can see large profits when the natural statistics give you a number of winners in a row. However, the opposite is also true. Leverage in an account can hurt you when the natural statistics give you a number of losers in a row.

This is why, before we get started, I want to share some of the lessons about trading I have learned during the last 20 years.

> There is no magic to trading. It is about putting the odds on your side—and not trading unless they are. This sounds simple, but it takes a few years to get good at it. And, like most things, while you are learning it is best to work with someone.

> The market will not adapt to us, we must adapt to it. Active trading when the market is in a narrow range presents higher than average risk. Traders can compensate for higher risk market conditions by trading fewer positions and using smaller position sizes. Failure to do this can be costly.

> Successful traders adjust their trading style, trading system, holding period, and exit strategies based on the current market conditions. This is a process I refer to as market adaptive trading. It is better to learn how to adapt to the market than to run from one trading idea to the next looking for the next super system.

> As a trader, I do not care which way the market moves. I can make money either way. It is important to be able to quickly react to whatever the market does and not be emotionally

attached to any particular choice. I cannot control what the market does, so I have a plan for whichever path it picks and then I trade the plan.

Always be thinking about taking and protecting profits.

If you are not sure what to do, exit the position. There will always be more trades to choose from.

You do not need to trade every day. Let the setups come to you and take the best ones. When the market is moving, there are lots of good setups to trade. If there are few setups, or most are failing, then listen to the message of the market.

Do not rush in. There is plenty of time to get into a tradable move when the market changes. If a trend is worth trading, then by definition you do not have to be in on the first day.

Never enter a position without a plan for exiting.

Do not count your chickens before they hatch. You do not have a profit until you are back in cash.

Never trade with money you cannot afford to lose.

Trading is not a team sport. Stay away from chat rooms and financial TV. Seek the truth, not support from others with your point of view.

Enjoy and Happy Trading!

—*Steve Palmquist*

—|FOREWORD|—

by Oliver L. Velez

I have the distinct pleasure of learning from the thousands of traders who have participated in my courses and programs. It has shown me that the challenges I faced learning to trade are the same challenges that all traders face. As I read through Steve Palmquist's book, *Money-Making Candlestick Patterns*, I noticed that it zeroed in on one of the toughest obstacles to profitable trading—conquering the odds. The most successful traders I have met have put in the time needed to comprehend how important it is to know their winning trade percentage. To fully understand how probability comes into play, let's start with a definition. Webster's defines trading as: "to engage in frequent buying and selling of (as stocks or commodities) usually in search of quick profits." Notice the key words that even Webster knew to include; "…in search of," nodding to the fact that 'quick profits' are ever so elusive.

To me, trading is "Using technical analysis to find a moment in time when the odds are in your favor. Then trading becomes a matter of your entry and management." In other words, it is having the knowledge to know when the odds are in your favor, having the patience to wait for that moment, then having the discipline to handle the trade properly when it goes in your favor and also handle it properly when goes against you."

Let's dissect a little. The opening words are "using technical analysis." Now, I know the Webster's definition would let you trade with fundamentals, but not mine. I have written extensively on this in my own books, but suffice it to say that the opening words are not a misprint. We begin our search on the charts. This is the only place where we find truth and useful information in the markets. Not from analysts, not from brokers, and not from accountants.

Next comes "a moment in time." How long is a moment in time? It depends on your time frame. For a core trader that moment may be a day, for a swing trader several minutes, for a day or scalp trader, perhaps only a few seconds. The point is that there is only one moment when that exact trade is proper. Any thing past that moment, and that trade is gone and if executed, wrong.

Next, when are "the odds in your favor?" Well, that comes down to a matter of knowledge and technical patterns. We are looking for the exact moment when a stock "shows its hand" and gives away a key secret—letting you in when a pattern or sudden event develops that appears to be something other than just random noise.

And it is at this critical point that Steve Palmquist has presented some of the most valuable research that I've seen in a long time. Let me explain further.

As you may know, charts of stocks, futures, indices, or any item that changes price over time can be drawn in a variety of ways. Line charts and bar charts are a couple of common ways. I use only Japanese candlestick charts and don't consider a chart complete without them.

The main difference between Japanese candlestick analysis and Western bar chart analysis is that the Japanese place the highest importance on the relationship between the open and close of the same period, while Westerners place the importance on the close as it relates to the prior period's close. While all of this data may be available on a Western bar chart, it is difficult to see quickly.

The candlesticks color each bar based on whether it closed above its open (white), or below it's open (black) so it is easy to tell who won the "battle" on that bar. Note that a candle may be closing under the prior candle and still be white, if it closed above its open. This could happen if the stock gapped down at open. Also keep in mind that as long as the underlying stock closes higher than the prior day's close, Western thought says it's positive; however, according to the Japanese view, this is not necessarily the case. If on an up day, the stock closes below its open, the Japanese would regard it as negative.

The high and low of the day are then seen as "tails" that stick out above or below the colored body. These are also called "wicks' as in the wick of a candle. A long tail at the top of the candle shows the bears were able to move the stock significantly, as the stock closed well off its high. A long tail at the bottom of the candle shows the bulls were able to move the stock significantly, as the stock closed well off its low.

The different shapes and colors that these candlesticks assume can help give an indication of what is happening with that stock. Several of these candlesticks in a row can give rise to possible patterns that often repeat, giving us tradable strategies.

One of the most notable books on the subject is *Japanese Candlestick Charting Techniques* by Steve Nison. But, what is amazing to me, is that even learning from the father of candlesticks himself, you run the risk of misinterpreting the definitions of these candlestick patterns. Often vague in description, the same candlestick pattern can be used differently by different traders for very different results. What Steve Palmquist hands you is his detailed research into how to best define the most popular candlestick patterns for less ambiguity and more profitability.

In chapter 1, he reviews the basic candlestick and the background into his testing methods. His knowledge on backtesting is vast and evident in the subsequent chapters on the bullish engulfing, bearish engulfing, hammer, hanging man, morning star, and evening star patterns. Each chapter breaks down the pattern to examine how different parameters impact results. In an organized and detailed manner, Steve presents the reader with the definitions that most often produce profitable trades.

However, some of the most important information is presented in the last chapter. This is where Steve introduces you to how to use his research; by implementing his unique system of trading, one he calls Market Adaptive Trading. It is in this chapter that he really pulls all of his research together and gives you a way to put it to work immediately. Proving that some patterns work better under certain market conditions, Steve will show you how to use candlesticks most effectively by using only the highest probability setups; truly, the key to trading.

To bring this full circle, let's finish dissecting the end of my personal definition of trading – "then it becomes a matter of entry and management." In other words, here is where the psychology comes in to play. Once you learn how, the intelligence actually required to enter and manage a trade is minimal. The ability to do so; is rare. This is where you become your own worst enemy, and is the level that even the most astute traders seldom pass. You must have the knowledge to know; the patience to wait; and the discipline to handle. Even with all of this research, it is ultimately up to us, the astute traders, to manage the trade properly. The goal, of course, is to increase the winners and minimize the losers. This book prepares you to do just that.

Here, Steve Palmquist gives you an immediate edge in the markets. Are you exploiting your edge on every trade you place? Do you even know what your edge is? The most experienced and successful market players know very well what their edge is and work to exploit that edge only if the opportunity arises. In the absence of a high odds opportunity, the successful market player will exercise patience and discipline and stay in cash. He or she does not become restless and trade (take risk) simply because they average three trades an hour, day or week (or five, or eight, etc.) and it is rapidly approaching the market closing time or weekend and they have placed no trades at all. Each day offers different odds. A successful market player with a proven edge will consider some of these events (which timeframe depends on your trading plan) to be opportunities and other events to be high risk setups only a sucker would play (or the novices, sheep, and dumb money).

Can you know with certainty that your next trade is a winner or loser? You can't. You can only extrapolate probabilities from the current setup and your past results and statistics. The successful market player specializes in certain well defined strategies and also tracks his/her trades extensively and mines the data for information. This is the very essence of *Money-Making Candlestick Patterns*. And this is exactly why this book will remain a valuable tool on my bookshelf for years to come.

—Olíver L. Velez, CEO

Velez Capital Management, LLC

Author of: *Strategies for Profiting on Every Trade, Tools and Tactics for the Master Day Trader* (with Greg Capra), and the *Swing Trading* and *Option Trading Tactics* Course Books.

MONEY-MAKING
CANDLESTICK
PATTERNS

Backtested for Proven Results

CHAPTER 1

CANDLESTICK BASICS AND TESTING REQUIREMENTS

Candlestick charting was developed in Japan about 300 years ago as traders noticed specific price patterns and began using them for forecasting price movements in the rice market. Japan had an active market in trading rice, and even rice futures, during the 1700s. Traders involved in this market noticed that certain patterns in price movements often preceded moves in the price of rice. They began to look for and study these patterns and to use them in determining whether to take positions.

While candlestick techniques have been used for hundreds of years in Japan, they are a relatively new tool for trading stocks in the West. It is thought that candlestick techniques started moving beyond a few pioneers in Western markets during the 1980s and gained popularity during the 1990s after the publication of several books on the subject, most notably Steve Nison's *Beyond Candlesticks: New Japanese Charting Techniques Revealed* and *Strategies for Profiting with Japanese Candlestick Charts*.

Some traders feel that candlestick patterns are mysterious and must be highly effective if they have been in use for hundreds of years; however, there are many products that have been around a long time and may or may not be effective. It's not the length of time something has been around that matters; it is whether it produces results. Some candlestick patterns are great tools; others are interesting but less effective. The trick for traders is to know which ones work best, and how to improve the others.

Many candlestick patterns were given names 300 years ago by the Japanese rice traders. The traders used the names to describe the pattern. Some, like the hammer pattern, look just like what the name suggests. Others seem a little less descriptive to Western traders. However, names of common Western patterns like island top, climax run, head and shoulders, and double top may also seem strange to new traders. The strangeness of the name is unusual at first, but soon becomes just a name as the trader studies and becomes familiar with the pattern.

In any case, a name is a name. It is the ability to recognize the pattern that is important. In this chapter, we will look at several popular candlestick patterns and then learn how and when to pull them from our toolbox and put them to use. But first, let's go over the basics.

WHAT IS A CANDLESTICK?

Candlestick patterns, like Western patterns, show relationships between the opening, closing, high, and low prices of a stock on one or more days. Bar charts and candlesticks are both constructed from the same information; they just display it in a slightly different manner.

A basic candlestick representation of each trading day looks like Figure 1.1. The rectangular area is the candlestick body and represents the distance or price change between the opening and the closing price for the day. If the stock moved up on the day, the candlestick body color is white. If the stock moved down, the candlestick body is black. The different body colors make it easy to glance at a candlestick chart and tell instantly if the stock was up or down for the day. If the stock is consistently moving up, you will see a chart with a lot of white bodies. If the stock is mostly moving down, you will see a chart with a lot of black bodies.

FIGURE 1.1:
BASIC CANDLESTICK REPRESENTATION
OF A DAY'S TRADING RESULTS

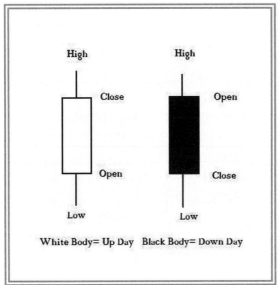

Shadow = + line above or below (handwritten note)

The thin lines on the top and bottom of the candlestick body are called shadows or tails. The end of the upper shadow shows the high price for the day, the end of the lower shadow shows the low price for the day. The day's trading range is the difference between the top of the upper shadow and the bottom of the lower shadow. Single day candlestick patterns are defined by the relationships between the size of the body and the two tails. Multi-day patterns are defined by the relationship of the body and shadow patterns across more than one day.

Candlestick patterns, like Western patterns, may be formed over one or more days. An island top can form in three days, a head and shoulders may form over several weeks. A hammer is a one day candlestick pattern, while a bullish engulfing pattern forms over two days. In general, patterns occurring over a few days may indicate short term direction, and patterns occurring over several weeks may indicate longer-term direction of prices. Now let's take a look at some of the more popular candlestick patterns. After learning these, we will investigate how often they work and what makes them effective.

HAMMER AND HANGING MAN CANDLESTICK PATTERNS

THE HAMMER

The hammer and hanging man patterns are identical and have long lower shadows, short or no upper shadows, and small bodies. The pattern, shown in Figure 1.2, is called a hammer if it occurs during a downtrend and a hanging man if it occurs during an uptrend. The color of the body is not important. The lower shadow should be twice the length of the body or more. There should be no or very little upper shadow, indicating that the day's high should be near the close for a white body and near the open for a black body.

FIGURE 1.2:
BASIC HAMMER AND HANGING MAN
CANDLESTICK PATTERNS

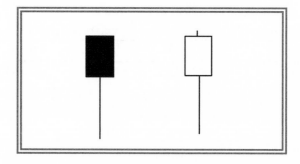

Figure 1.3 shows a candlestick chart of BBH. BBH had been in a clear downtrend during January, February, and the first part of March 2007. On 03/14/07, BBH formed a hammer pattern as marked by the up arrow. The hammer pattern marked the end of the downtrend, and BBH rose more than seven points during the next five sessions. Obviously, not every hammer

pattern is a profitable trade. The important question for traders is: how often does the pattern result in profitable trades, and are there other factors that influence the results? These questions can be answered by using backtesting techniques to examine the results of thousands of trades.

FIGURE 1.3:
CANDLESTICK CHART WITH HAMMER PATTERN

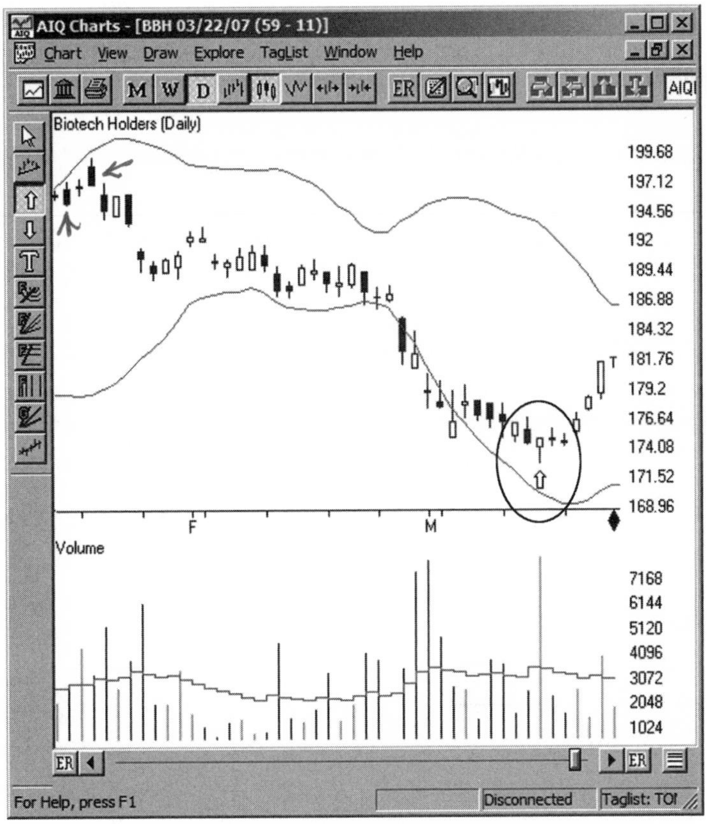

Courtesy of AIQ

Chapter four will focus on trading the hammer pattern and address questions that successful traders must know the answers to:

- What constitutes a small upper shadow?
- How does the shadow length affect trading results?

- How do closing price and volume affect trading results?
- Does the size of the day's trading range affect the results of trading hammers?

THE HANGING MAN

Figure 1.4 shows a candlestick chart of NEU during the first half of 2006. On 05/09/06, NEU formed a hanging man pattern as marked by the up arrow in Figure 1.4. The hanging man pattern marked the end of the uptrend in NEU and subsequently, it declined nearly 12 points during the next four trading sessions.

FIGURE 1.4:
CANDLESTICK CHART WITH HANGING MAN PATTERN

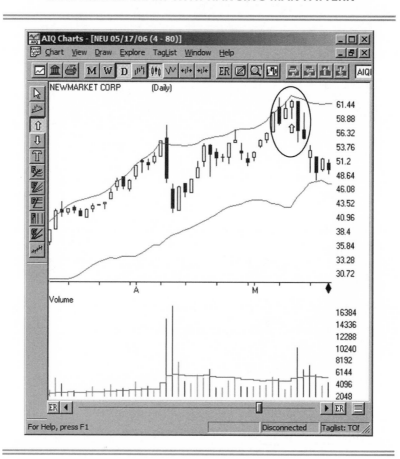

Courtesy of AIQ

When traders get together and discuss trading patterns or setups, someone usually asks why a particular pattern works. To explain trading patterns, the market is often described as a battle between the bulls trying to drive prices up, and the bears trying to drive prices down. The patterns are the result of this contest between the bulls and bears. In the case of a hammer pattern, the stock has been in a downtrend, indicating that the bears have control. When the hammer forms, the price is initially driven down further by the bears, forming the long lower tail. At some point during the day, the bulls step in and drive the price back up near the opening, forming the small body. The hammer forms at a point where bullish investors are willing to step in; therefore, the downtrend ends and the stock begins to move up.

Some traders will start using a pattern or trading system when they hear an explanation of why it works that makes sense to them. We all have a need to understand why something should work. However, for traders, it is more important to know how often a pattern works rather than an explanation of why it works. Knowing why a pattern works is interesting. Knowing how often a trading pattern works can be profitable. And, knowing in what specific market conditions a pattern works best can be very profitable. In the next chapter we will address these issues and develop a working knowledge of when to use candlestick patterns and when to use another tool from the trading toolbox.

Chapter five will look at issues related to trading the hanging man pattern including:

- How do bullish or bearish market environments affect trading results for the hanging man pattern?
- What happens if the pattern occurs on the recent highs of the move?
- Does using the MACD for timing improve results?
- Does waiting for confirmation improve results?
- How long should a position be held?

BULLISH AND BEARISH
ENGULFING CANDLESTICK PATTERNS

BULLISH ENGULFING

The hammer and hanging man candlestick patterns occur in a single day. Engulfing patterns take two days to form and focus on the relationship between the candlestick bodies of both days. The candlestick shadows are not important to defining the pattern. A bullish engulfing pattern occurs when the white body of the second candlestick engulfs or covers the black body of the first candlestick in the pattern as shown in Figure 1.5. A bearish engulfing pattern occurs when the black body of the second day engulfs or covers the white body of the first day.

FIGURE 1.5:
BASIC ENGULFING PATTERNS

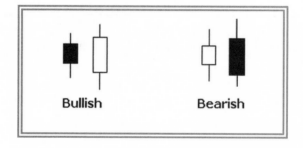

The bullish engulfing pattern is a reversal pattern formed when the stock is in a downtrend, and often signals a short term reversal or bounce in the stock price. The first candlestick in this two day pattern has a black body, indicating the bearish downtrend is still intact. Black bodies indicate the stock closed down for the day. The second candlestick has a white body extending below the first day's body, indicating the stock gapped down at the open. The lower end of a black body is the day's closing price, and the lower end of a white body is the day's opening price. Thus, when the second day's white body engulfs or covers the first day's black body, the price gaps down in the morning indicating more bearishness, then reverses to close above the previous day's opening, indicating a reversal in sentiment for the second day that often continues in the short term.

Figure 1.6 shows a four-month candlestick chart of ZION. During late June and early July of 2006, ZION was in a clear downtrend. On July 13 and July 14, it formed the two day bullish engulfing pattern as marked by the up arrows. During the five days following the formation of the bullish engulfing pattern, ZION ran up more than seven points.

FIGURE 1.6:
ZION BULLISH ENGULFING PATTERN OF 7/14/06

Courtesy of AIQ

The bullish engulfing pattern does not always mark the end of a downtrend, but often does. Trading is a statistical business and patterns do not work all the time. Some trading patterns yield positive results a significant percentage of the time. Using trading patterns that win more often than they lose can be profitable in the long run. One of the keys to trading is to understand which patterns and techniques to use and in what market conditions they will be effective. That's what this book is all about. Traders need to understand how often a pattern produces profits and how often it generates losses, and then fill their trading toolboxes with techniques that are profitable more often than random chance.

The bullish engulfing pattern is examined in more detail in chapter two where we look at the effects of several parameters on the trading results for bullish engulfing patterns including:

- Test results in multiple time periods.
- Test results in bullish and bearish market environments.
- Effect of stock price and volume on trading results.
- Effect of second day volume spike on trading results.
- Effect of using a 50 period moving average filter on trading results.
- Effect of upper shadow size on trading results.

BEARISH ENGULFING

A bearish engulfing pattern may occur after a stock has been in an uptrend. The first day of this two day pattern shows a white body, indicating the stock was still moving up. The second day of the pattern has a black body that completely covers or engulfs the body of the previous day. The top of the black body represents the opening price, which has gapped up, since it is above the top of the previous day's body, which represented the closing price for the first day of the pattern. After the open on the second day, the stock may move up further depending on whether the second day's candlestick has a top shadow or tail. Because the second day is a black candle, it means that at some point during the day the sentiment reversed and the price started declining. This change in sentiment could signal a further decline in the short term.

Figure 1.7 shows a candlestick chart for CRS, which was in an uptrend during February, March, April, and early May of 2006. It formed a bearish engulfing pattern on 05/11/06, as marked by the two down arrows. After the formation of the two day pattern, the stock dropped more than 25 points. The bearish

FIGURE 1.7:
CRS BEARISH ENGULFING PATTERN OF 05/11/06

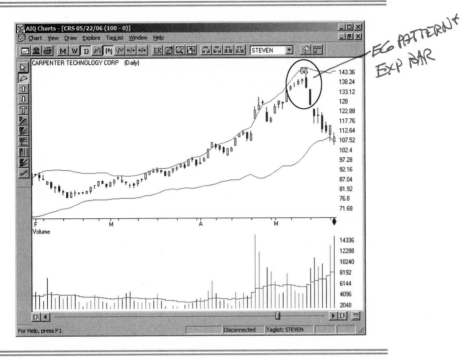

Courtesy of AIQ

engulfing pattern marked a clear and decisive end to the uptrend. In this case, traders would have profited by entering short positions in CRS after the bearish engulfing pattern formed and then covering just seven sessions later.

In addition to knowing how often a particular trading pattern produces profitable trades, traders should understand if there are observable parameters that can strongly influence results.

Some of the questions traders should address before using a trading pattern are:

- How long should a position be held?
- What are good profit target points?
- What type of orders should be used?

• Where should stop loss orders be entered?

These and other issues affecting trading results will be addressed in chapter three.

MORNING AND EVENING STAR PATTERNS

MORNING STAR

The morning star pattern is a three bar pattern that marks the end, or reversal, of a downtrend. The first bar is a long black body that indicates a continuation of the downtrend. The second bar features a small body, which can be either black or white, and gaps lower. The third day of the pattern shows a white body that closes well within the area of the first day's black body. Figure 1.8 shows a basic morning star pattern.

FIGURE 1.8:
BASIC MORNING STAR PATTERN

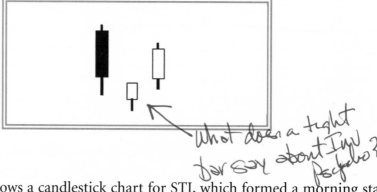

What does a tight bar say about supply?

Figure 1.9 shows a candlestick chart for STI, which formed a morning star pattern on 04/13/07. STI had been in a downtrend and formed a large black body on 04/11/07. The following day, STI showed a small white body that gapped lower, and on the final day of the three day pattern, the morning star was completed by the formation of the large white body marked by the

FIGURE 1.9:
MORNING STAR PATTERN IN STI ON 4/13/07

Courtesy of AIQ

down arrow. The morning star pattern marked the end of the downtrend, and STI rose nearly 10% over the next few days.

Chapter six examines the effects of altering each of the parameters of this three day trading pattern in order to determine what works best; these include:

- Effect of candlestick body size on trading results.
- What constitutes a "small body" on day two of the pattern?
- Effect of market conditions on trading results.
- Does the color of the day two body matter?
- Performance in multi-year test periods.

EVENING STAR

The evening star is a three bar reversal pattern that may signal the end of a stock's uptrend. The first candlestick in the pattern has a long white body, indicating the current uptrend is continuing. The second candlestick in the evening star pattern gaps up and then forms a small body. The distance between the open and close is not very large, as if the enthusiasm of the initial opening gap up cannot be maintained. The third candle in the pattern is a black candle indicating a reversal of sentiment, and the black candle must close at least halfway down the range of the first day's candlestick. The basic evening star pattern is shown in Figure 1.10.

FIGURE 1.10:
BASIC EVENING STAR PATTERN

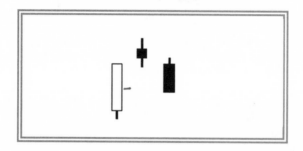

Figure 1.11 shows a candlestick chart for ADBE, which was in an uptrend during April of 2006. The uptrend ended with the formation of an evening star pattern on 05/01/06. On the first day of the pattern, ADBE formed a long white bar, followed by a gap up and a narrow-bodied black bar on the next day. The pattern was completed on the third day, when ADBE formed a large black bar that closed well into the range of the first day. Following the formation of the evening star pattern, ADBE dropped more than 10% over the next few days.

Chapter seven examines the evening star pattern in more detail in order to determine how the various parameters in the definition affect trading results.

FIGURE 1.11:
EVENING STAR PATTERN IN ADBE ON 5/01/06

Significant? Probl need longer uptrend? Over 250.

EB? Indicates a reversal?

EB

INDICATES REVERSAL?

 # — does a tight pattern mean anything? Inv sentiment balanced?

Courtesy of AIQ

EB+1 might be workable?

These include:

- The effects of a very low day three in the pattern.
- The effect of a long day three body.
- Does a gap down on day three affect the trading results?
- What is the effect of white space gaps on trading results?
- What is the effect of various day two body size requirements?
- What exactly constitutes a "big" body on the first day of the pattern?

TESTING CANDLESTICK PATTERNS

Candlestick patterns can be effective tools for the trader's toolbox; however, like any other tool, the user needs to understand exactly what it is designed for and how to use it effectively. Carpenters can make beautiful things with a table saw, but they have to know how to use it and when another tool might be more appropriate for the task at hand. They also need to know the safety rules, how to avoid kickback, and the importance of using a push tool. At least the carpenters that still have all their fingers do.

The analogy holds for trading patterns. There are times when a particular candlestick pattern is effective, and times when another candlestick pattern should be used to do the job. Trading any pattern, candlesticks or some other technique, without a clear understanding of what it is and what to expect in different situations is like using a power tool without an understanding of its use and safety precautions. To protect your fingers and your money, it is a good idea to have a clear understanding of how the tools you are using work.

It is not unusual for trading patterns to have undefined or unclear parameters. Some patterns, such as the hammer, have specifications that may be interpreted differently by different traders. The same is true for Western patterns such as flags and the head and shoulders pattern. The hammer pattern requires, "little or no upper shadow." The definition of "little" will be interpreted differently by individual traders. This is one reason that several traders using the "same" pattern may see different results. One way to address this is to study the results of many trades using different lengths of upper shadows and then to compare the results. This process results in a clear definition of what constitutes "little upper shadow" and has the added benefit of giving the trader an indication of the type of results the pattern may produce.

Some traders gain a better understanding of trading patterns, and the environments in which to use them, though experience. After trading for a number of years, they begin to understand which variations of a particular trading pattern work best, and which ones are more prone to failure. Experience often produces good results when we are listening closely; however, it can be costly.

The Tidal Force of the Market

The overall market has a strong effect on how well trading patterns perform. Focusing solely on the patterns or setups in the individual stocks that you are trading can diminish results or make them highly variable. This is another reason why traders using the same patterns may experience different results. Trading patterns are like waves at the beach; they all are affected by the tide.

Even when the tide is going out, there are waves coming in, just as there is usually something moving up even in bearish market conditions. Like conditions at high tide, when the market is bullish, we are likely to see more stocks moving up. Using different trading tools designed for specific market conditions is a process I call market adaptive trading (MAT), which we will cover in the last chapter.

In order to develop the tools and techniques for market adaptive trading, one has to be able to analyze a number of different trading tools in various market conditions and determine which are the most effective in specific market environments. After doing this, a trader can look at the market to determine the current environment, then open the trading toolbox and select the appropriate tools. Without this knowledge, the trader may be using the wrong tool, which could lead to significant drawdowns and wide account swings.

I believe a less expensive way to develop an in-depth understanding of how trading patterns work is by backtesting the pattern. Backtesting allows us to test how simple variations or changes in the trading pattern affect results. Backtesting can be done during a variety of time periods and even in specific market conditions.

You do not have to become a software engineer to backtest candlestick patterns; there are several good products available that provide backtesting tools traders can use. In fact, most of the available choices provide excellent results and probably more statistics than the average trader may care about. All of my backtesting results shown in the subsequent chapters were produced using AIQ Systems' Trading Expert Pro. The analysis can also be done with other backtesting tools; the important thing is to make sure to do the analysis before trading a system with hard-earned money.

WHY BACKTEST?

Backtesting allows traders to see how a system has performed in the past, to evaluate different filters and parameters, and to evaluate a system in different market conditions. Backtesting is not a guarantee of future performance. Successful backtesting requires an ability to describe the trading pattern in a backtesting language, knowledge of appropriate testing periods, an understanding of how to interpret the results, and an ability to add and test different filters or parameters to the original test description.

HOW DOES BACKTESTING WORK?

The process of describing the trading pattern in a backtesting language varies depending on which program is being used. Each software package has its advantages and disadvantages. The key is to select one that is easy to understand and use. More power and features are a waste if you cannot figure them out.

Backtesting results are typically presented in a format similar to that shown in Figure 1.12. The results in Figure 1.12 provide a lot of information, including the number of winning and losing trades, maximum profit and loss, average drawdown, the probability of winning and losing trades, annualized ROI, and other factors. It is usually not necessary to absorb all these numbers—there are really just four things that matter. The rest is interesting but not vital.

```
Effective Candlestick Patterns - Expert Design Studio                    _ □ ×
File  Test  View  Help

 □ A'   □ 🖙 🖫 🖨 🖳 🗚              ! ● ☑ ■
Summary | Positions |

BasicBullishEngulfing
                                          Winners       Losers       Neutral
                                        ==========   ==========   ==========
Number of trades in test:        3087        1671         1394           22
Average periods per trade:       7.25        7.28         7.22         7.14

Maximum Profit/Loss:                       31.76 %     (29.23)%
Average Drawdown:              (2.34)%      (0.89)%      (4.11)%
Average Profit/Loss:            0.48 %       3.73 %      (3.40)%
Average SPX Profit/Loss:        0.35 %       0.80 %      (0.18)%

Probability:                               54.13 %      45.16 %
Average Annual ROI:            24.35 %     187.07 %    (171.80)%
Annual SPX (Buy & Hold):       14.34 %

Reward/Risk Ratio:              1.32

Start test date:             01/03/06
End test date:               05/01/07

Interval: Daily
Pricing Summary
   Entry price: [Open]
   Exit price: [Open]
Exit Summary
   Hold for 5 periods

For Help, press F1                                            NUM
```

Courtesy of AIQ

The four key things to look for in backtesting results are:

- The number of trades in the test period.
- The annualized ROI.
- The percentage of winning trades.
- The percentage profit/loss of the average winning/losing trade.

The number of trades in the test period gives you an idea of how valid the test results might be, and whether it is worth trading. A trading pattern that only produces a few trades a year may be due to seasonal or news factors and not the pattern itself. A trading pattern that produces 100 trades a year is more likely to be due to the characteristics of the pattern itself, and, therefore, has a better chance of recurring in the future.

The annualized ROI provides an indication of how well the trading pattern performs. Since the number is usually calculated by taking the percentage gain for a trade during the holding period and then annualizing the result, it can exaggerate the returns of patterns with short holding periods that do not occur very often. This is rarely the percentage return traders will see in their account because many traders cannot take all the trades generated by a trading pattern, and the calculation does not include slippage and transaction fees. The ROI number is best used as a figure of merit; more is generally better. Annualized ROI is like the gas mileage numbers posted in a car dealership—you know you will not get that exact mileage, but bigger numbers are generally better than smaller ones.

The percentage of winning trades for a trading pattern is important. If the average profit on a winning trade is larger than the average loss on a losing trade, then, in general, the more often the pattern produces a winning trade, the better the results. Imagine we are going to flip a coin 100 times, and every time it comes up heads, you give me $1.50; and, when it comes up tails, I give you $1.20. Over the long run, I expect the outcome to be profitable for me, and frankly hope you will continue to play.

The odds for each coin flip are 50/50 for heads. I do not know if any particular coin flip will be profitable for me; but, since I expect to win about half the time, and since I get paid more when I win than I have to pay when I lose, I should make a profit in the long run. Trading patterns are similar in that you do not know the outcome of any particular trade; but, if your odds of a winning trade are better than 50/50, and you make more on the average winner than you lose on the average loser, you would expect to make money in the long run.

Trading patterns should have an advantage over coin flipping; they should provide winning trades more than half the time. This stacks the odds in the trader's favor. If a trading pattern wins more than 50% of the time, and the average winning trade gains more than the average losing trade loses, then trading is a better game than the coin flip example. The stock pattern trader still does not know if any given trade will be profitable, but over the long run, the odds are favorable for the net result to be profitable. Traders do not focus on the results of any one trade, they focus on whether or not the account balance is going up over the long run.

FIGURE 1.13:
NASDAQ MONTHLY CHART 1994 TO 2007

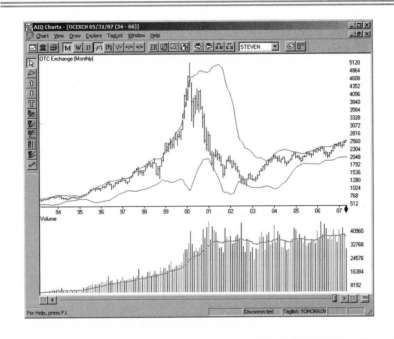

Courtesy of AIQ

WHAT TIME FRAME DO I USE?

While backtesting can yield great insight into how candlestick patterns perform and the risks associated with particular trading patterns, they need to be run over a specific time frame. Choosing that time frame can be confusing. Many people initially feel that the longer the time frame of the backtest, the better the results. Figure 1.13 illustrates why there is a better way to select time frames for backtesting.

Figure 1.13 shows the NASDAQ market over a 14-year period. If backtesting is done over a specific time period, then one is assuming that the next period of similar length will be just like the previous period. If one tests a trading pattern over the 2004 to 2007 period and uses the results to trade in 2007 to 2010, the trader is expecting the 2007 through 2010 period to look similar to the 2004 through 2007 period. This may at first seem reasonable, but further examination of Figure 1.13 reveals that it is hard to find two four-year periods that look just like each other.

The market is always changing; we do not know what it will look like in the future. There is one constant though: Each market time frame is made from a collection of bullish, bearish, and trading range periods. The market is either going up, down, or sideways. It is impossible for it to do anything else. This indicates that trading patterns should be tested in each of the three conditions, and then traders should select the patterns that they have found to be most effective during the current conditions. Yes, testing a trading pattern over a calendar time frame is also good. But use more than one time period and also look at performance in each of the three types of market conditions to gain a better understanding of how a potential trading system performs and when to use it.

TRADING IS A STATISTICAL BUSINESS—RISK MANAGEMENT

The probability of a winning trade not only provides insight into whether a trading pattern is worth using, it also provides insight into position sizing and money management strategies. In the coin flip example, few people would want to bet their entire account on each trade because to come out ahead, they would need to win every coin flip. The more times the coin is flipped, the more likely it becomes they would lose their entire account. The same is true for trading.

If a trading pattern has a 50% chance of producing a winning trade, then the likelihood of eight losing trades in a row is one in 256. These seem like good odds against losing eight times in a row, unless you also consider how many trades the trader makes in a year. If the trader makes 50 trades a year, the trader is unlikely to see eight losing trades in a row and might consider risking 1/8 of the account on each trade. If another trader makes five trades a week, the odds are quite good that sometime during the year, he will see eight losing trades in a row. If the second trader risks 1/8 of the account on each trade, he has a good chance of going broke at some point during the year.

The amount risked on each trade should be a function of the probability of a winning trade, the number of trades made during the year, and the maximum drawdown the trader is willing to accept. Each trader has a different tolerance for risk. Some are bothered by a 10% drawdown in their account. Others do not lose sleep when experiencing a 30% drawdown. In this example, if each trader makes about 200 trades a year (and thus has a reasonable chance of seeing eight losing trades in a row), the first trader should risk less than 10% of his or her account divided by eight on each trade. The second trader should risk less than 30% of the account divided by eight.

The amount of risk, or maximum drawdown, a trader is willing to take divided by the maximum number of expected losses (which is a function of the number of trades made) is a starting point for considering the amount to risk on each trade. There are no guarantees in trading, but understanding how the winning percentage of the trading pattern and the number of trades affects overall risk is an important place to start when looking at risk management.

New traders often do not understand the risks they are taking and will blame drawdowns on bad luck, and then credit profits with their expertise at picking good trades. But always remember, trading is a statistical business. There is no magic indicator that will tell you which trades will work and which will not, no matter what those slick brochures say. Traders must understand the probabilities involved and how to use them to manage risk. The backtesting results are one way to gather some of this information.

Imagine 16 traders all using a trading pattern that wins half the time and yields 10% on each winning trade. If they all make a trade, we could expect eight traders to have winning trades with their accounts up 10%, and eight traders to have losing trades with their accounts down 10%. After the second trade, four traders would have winning trades both times and be up 20%. After four trades, there would be typically one trader who was up 40% and one who was down 40%.

The trader up 40% may be invited to speak on one of the financial programs "because he knows how to pick winners." The one down 40% would "just know" that the trading pattern did not work and may move on to another technique in an endless search for something better. Most of the traders would have results in the middle. Trading patterns that have winning trades more than 50% of the time and larger average wins than average losses move the odds significantly in the trader's advantage. Making actual trades is the easy part of trading; most of the work goes into researching and carefully understanding how a trading pattern performs.

Traders want to use trading patterns that have winning percentages well above 50% because it stacks the odds in their favor. They also want the average winner to yield more than the average loser costs them. When these two conditions are met, the trader knows that the inevitable winning streaks should gain more than the inevitable losing streaks lose, and also the winning streaks should happen more often than the losing streaks. It is this knowledge that makes trading worthwhile. As is true with every business, knowledge is one of the keys to success in trading.

Trading without this knowledge exposes you to unknown risks. Traders with a clear understanding of how different trading patterns perform are willing to take known risks for expected gains. There is a connection between the level of risk assumed and the expected returns. Lower risks can be easier to tolerate, but often result in lower returns. Higher risks expose the trader to larger drawdowns, and potentially larger gains. Each trader needs to find the risk/reward scenario that is most comfortable for them.

CHAPTER 2

BULLISH ENGULFING PATTERNS

L et's review. The bullish engulfing pattern is a reversal pattern formed in downtrending stocks and often signals a short term reversal or bounce in the stock price. The first candlestick in this two day pattern has a black body, indicating the bearish downtrend is still intact. Black bodies indicate the stock closed down for the day. The second candlestick has a white body extending below the first day's body, indicating the stock gapped down at the open. The lower end of a black body is the day's closing price and the lower end of a white body is the day's opening price. Thus, when the second day's white body engulfs or covers the first day's black body, the price gaps down in the morning, indicating more bearishness. It then reverses to close above the previous day's opening, indicating a reversal in sentiment for the second day. This often continues in the short term.

Figure 2.1 shows a bullish engulfing candlestick pattern that developed in CYBX on 05/19/06. CYBX had been in a three-week downtrend, which fulfills the first requirement for the pattern. The first day of this two day pattern was the black-bodied candlestick on 05/18/06. The black body indicated a down day for CYBX, which was a continuation of the current downtrend. The next day was a white-bodied candlestick (marked by the up arrow) in which both the upper and lower ends of the candlestick body overlap or engulf the body of the previous day's candlestick.

The bullish engulfing pattern marked the end of the downtrend for CYBX and, during the next five trading sessions, it ran up nearly 30%. A 30% profit in a few days helps keep food on the table, but traders need to know more than just whether a pattern has worked. They need to know how reliable it is—how *often* it works.

FIGURE 2.1:
CYBX BULLISH ENGULFING PATTERN OF 5/19/06

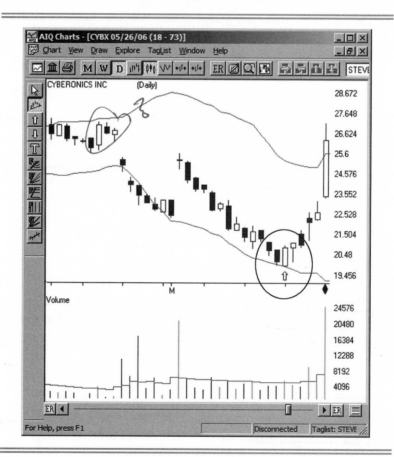

Courtesy of AIQ

+ in itself should be bearish

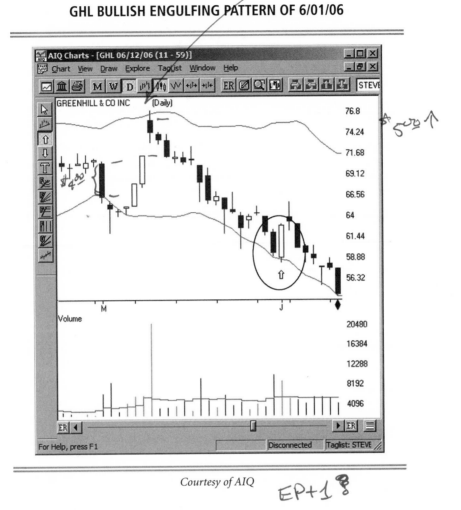

$5 → ↑

$4.90

Courtesy of AIQ   EP+1 ?

Figure 2.2 shows a bullish engulfing pattern that occurred in GHL during a three-week downtrend. The pattern occurred on 06/01/06 and is marked by an up arrow in Figure 2.2. If a trader had entered a long position the day after the bullish engulfing pattern formed, he or she would have seen a 10 point loss during the next six sessions.

If trading patterns worked all the time, trading would be easy and everyone would be doing it. We have all seen marketing pieces promising secret knowledge of a super trading system that offers 1,000% returns. The truth is there are no trading systems producing a reasonable number of trades that win all the time in the long run. One of the tricks to trading is to have a variety of trading patterns that work most of the time and to know how to select the best patterns for the current market conditions. Candlestick patterns provide a number of opportunities along these lines.

Definition is the first step in unlocking the secrets of trading bullish engulfing patterns; let's review the bullish engulfing pattern.

BULLISH ENGULFING PATTERN—STANDARD DEFINITION

- The stock must be in a downtrend.
- The first day of the pattern must be a black body candlestick.
- The second day of the pattern must be a white body candlestick.

- The second day's open must be less than the first day's close.
- The second day's close must be greater than the first day's close.

DETERMINING PATTERN EFFECTIVENESS

In order to understand how often the bullish engulfing candlestick pattern works, we could look at 100 charts during the last year and count the number of patterns that worked and the number that failed. This would give us a better understanding of how effective the pattern was during the last year. However, the manual approach quickly becomes impractical when, after looking at the data, we ask questions such as:

- Do the results change when looking at several hundred or 1,000 stocks?
- Do the results change when looking at a one-, two- or five-year test period?
- What is the win/loss ratio when the market is in bullish periods?
- Does the win/loss ratio change when the market is in bearish or trading range periods?
- Does it help to combine this candlestick pattern with other indicators?

- Does it make a difference if the stock is above or below a key moving average?
- Does it matter how much the second day's body overlaps the first day's body?
- Does the size of the body on either the first or second day of the pattern affect results?
- How long do I hold the position after entering?
- Does it matter if the volume on the second day of the pattern is higher or lower than the first day's volume?
- Does it matter if the volume is above or below average?
- Does the price of the stock affect the trading results?
- Does the average volume of the stock affect trading results?

In order to answer these questions, we would need to examine and record thousands of patterns in thousands of stocks, which could result in years of rather boring and methodical work. For a long time, this was a barrier to all but the most serious traders because of the extensive and repetitive work involved. Many traders would just trade patterns and hope for the best, but hope is not a trading strategy.

Fortunately, much of this work can be done easily on a good desktop computer with an investment of a few days' worth of time to learn how to use one of the backtesting software packages available to individual investors. The investment in, and the use of, this software is well worth it and can drastically reduce the effort required to answer trading questions like those outlined previously.

UNDERSTANDING THE LANGUAGE OF BACKTESTING

To unlock the secrets of this candlestick pattern, we also must translate each of the statements in the bullish engulfing pattern definition into statements of the backtesting language. Don't worry, the focus of this book is on results; but, I want to show an example of how easy it is to set up a backtest, and then focus on how to gather specific information that can be used to improve trading results. For more information on backtesting and developing trading ideas, you can also go to my website, www.daisydogger.com.

The definition of a downtrend is a series of lower highs and lower lows. When looking at a chart, the prices are declining as you move from the left to the right side of the chart. Using the AIQ Systems' Expert Design Studio (EDS), we can easily find a list of downtrending stocks with one simple EDS statement:

LOWERCLOSES IF HIVAL([CLOSE],5) < LOVAL([CLOSE],20,15)

LowerCloses is the name given to the list of downtrending stocks the computer will find for us. The EDS statement above instructs the computer to generate a list of all stocks that have the highest value in the last five trading sessions {HiVal([close],5)} less than the lowest value over a four-week period starting three weeks ago. The net result of this is a list of stocks whose current prices have declined recently. Traders can add a variety of refinements to this simple technique of finding downtrending stocks, but simple is usually a good place to start when dealing with computers.

The second part of the bullish engulfing definition is that the first day of the pattern must be a black body. A black body occurs by definition when the closing value of the stock is less than the day's opening value. This is expressed in the EDS testing language as:

BLACKBAR IF [CLOSE] < [OPEN]

The third part of the bullish engulfing definition is that the second day of the pattern must be a white body, which implies that the day's closing value must be higher than the day's opening value. This is expressed in the EDS language as:

WHITEBAR IF [CLOSE] > [OPEN]

The fourth part of the pattern is that the second day's open must be less than the first day's close. This is the requirement that places the lower part of the second day's body below the bottom of the first day's body. This is expressed in the EDS language as:

BOTTOMBODYOVERLAP IF [OPEN] < VAL([CLOSE],1)

The fifth part of the pattern requires the second day's closing value to be greater than the first day's close. This requirement places the upper part of the second day's white body above the upper part of the first day's black body. This is expressed in the EDS language as:

TOPBODYOVERLAP IF [CLOSE] > VAL([OPEN],1)

Combining the five parts of the bullish engulfing pattern description together results in the simple EDS program shown in Table 2.1 that can be used to find basic bullish engulfing patterns. It is a lot easier to find candlestick patterns using this computer scan than trying to look through 2,500 charts by hand. If you are interested in a copy of this EDS program, as well as the others used in the research for this book, e-mail a request to: candlestick@ daisydogger.com, or go to www.traderslibrary.com/TLECorner.

This EDS program is presented as an example of how quickly a variety of trading pattern scans can be developed. It is the kind of tool that was used to research the candlestick patterns discussed in this book. It is not necessary to fully understand how the EDS program works any more than it is necessary to understand how an internal combustion engine works in order to drive a car. The advantage of having the EDS program is that in a few seconds you can find all the bullish engulfing patterns that occurred on any given day, and you can evaluate the effectiveness of the pattern and various modifications to it.

SETTING UP THE INITIAL TEST

The EDS file of Table 2.1 can also be used for backtesting the bullish engulfing pattern. The backtesting process has the computer examine each and every setup that occurs in a given time frame and then determine the outcome of taking a trade based on each pattern that occurs. The backtesting program displays a number of statistics for both winning and losing trades that help the trader determine if the system being tested is worth risking real money on. Backtesting does not guarantee future performance of any system, but it does provide very useful insights into how effective a trading system might be.

TABLE 2.1.
BULLISH ENGULFING PATTERN EDS FILE

DownTrend if HiVal([close],5) < LoVal([close],20,15).

BlackBodyYesterday if val([close],1) < val([open],1).

WhiteBody if [close] > [open] .

BottomBodyOverlap if [open] < val([close],1).

TopBodyOverlap if [close] > val([open],1).

BasicBullishEngulfing if DownTrend and BlackBodyYesterday and
WhiteBody and BottomBodyOverlap and TopBodyOverlap.

In order to run a backtest, we need to have a clearly defined trading pattern, an entry strategy, an exit strategy, and a time period in which to test. Some trading patterns involve setup conditions followed by trigger conditions that specify whether to enter a position. In the case of the bullish engulfing pattern, the entry strategy is simply to take a position at the next trading session's opening price after the pattern forms. The initial exit strategy will simply be to hold the position for five days and then sell at the following session's opening price.

INITIAL TIME FRAME OF FOUR MONTHS

The initial test period will be the first four months of 2007. When running the first test on a trading idea, it is often a good idea just to try it over a short period to see if there is any merit to the idea. If it shows some promise, then more extensive testing can be done in a variety of different time periods and market conditions. The results of entering a long position the day after a bullish engulfing pattern formed, holding for five days, and then selling at the next day's opening price are shown in Figure 2.3.

Figure 2.3 shows some very interesting results. First of all, there were 691 bullish engulfing patterns during this four-month period, which indicates that the pattern is common and that there are plenty of trading opportunities. Patterns that occur rarely are difficult to rely on because there may not be a statistically significant number of tests from which to draw conclusions. The other problem with rare patterns is that as you add filters to them or test them in specific market conditions, they may become even rarer. The bullish engulfing pattern happens frequently enough that we do not need to worry about these issues.

The next interesting part of Figure 2.3 is that the bullish engulfing pattern resulted in a winning trade 62% of the time during this period. This number is very important—in general, the higher the winning percentage, the better. If we bet a dollar on a coin flip, the odds of winning are 50%. Over a large number of coin flips, the odds are we would come out even. In the case of

FIGURE 2.3:
BASIC BULLISH ENGULFING BACKTEST 1/1/07 TO 5/1/07

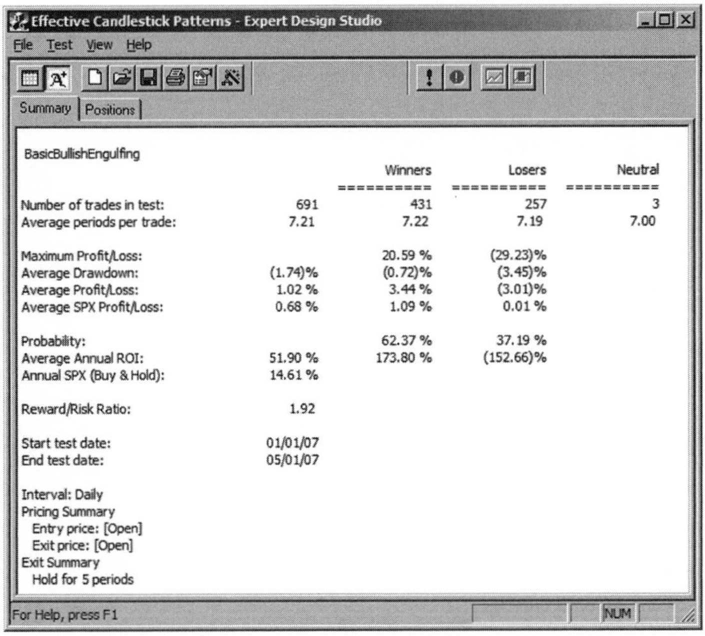

BasicBullishEngulfing

		Winners	Losers	Neutral
Number of trades in test:	691	431	257	3
Average periods per trade:	7.21	7.22	7.19	7.00
Maximum Profit/Loss:		20.59 %	(29.23)%	
Average Drawdown:	(1.74)%	(0.72)%	(3.45)%	
Average Profit/Loss:	1.02 %	3.44 %	(3.01)%	
Average SPX Profit/Loss:	0.68 %	1.09 %	0.01 %	
Probability:		62.37 %	37.19 %	
Average Annual ROI:	51.90 %	173.80 %	(152.66)%	
Annual SPX (Buy & Hold):	14.61 %			
Reward/Risk Ratio:	1.92			
Start test date:	01/01/07			
End test date:	05/01/07			

Interval: Daily
Pricing Summary
Entry price: [Open]
Exit price: [Open]
Exit Summary
Hold for 5 periods

Courtesy of AIQ

bullish engulfing patterns during this four-month period, if we took all the trades, we would have made a profit 62% of the time and lost money 37% of the time. These odds are much better than chance, and if they hold up under subsequent tests, then this would be an interesting pattern for traders.

The third intriguing part of Figure 2.3 is the average annualized ROI of 51%. If we had bought and sold the SPX on the same days we traded bullish engulfing patterns, the annualized ROI would have been only 14%. Now annualizing returns can be misleading because this assumes we took all 691 trades, which may not be possible in some accounts. For these reasons, I tend to look at the annualized return more as a figure of merit rather than an expected gain. More is usually better and traders should expect their trading patterns to have a higher annualized return than the SPX in order for the patterns to be worth trading.

FIGURE 2.4:
BASIC BULLISH ENGULFING BACKTEST JANUARY '06 TO MAY '07

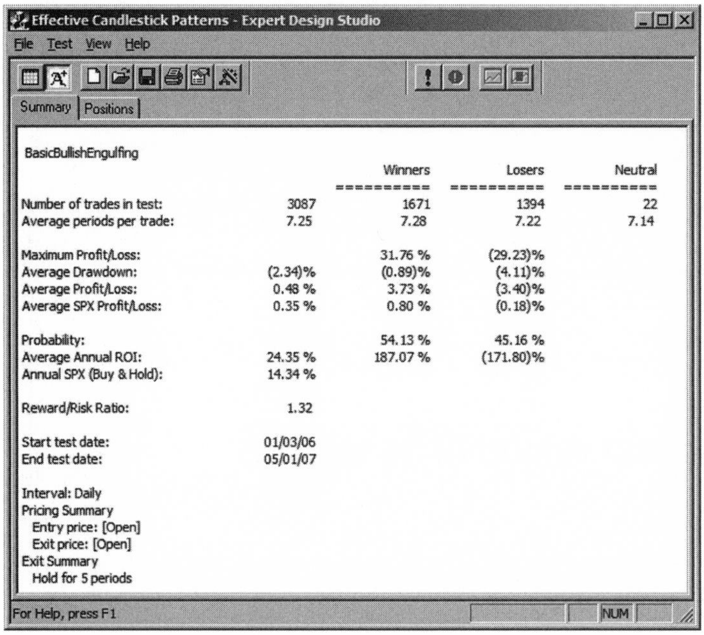

BasicBullishEngulfing

		Winners	Losers	Neutral
Number of trades in test:	3087	1671	1394	22
Average periods per trade:	7.25	7.28	7.22	7.14
Maximum Profit/Loss:		31.76 %	(29.23)%	
Average Drawdown:	(2.34)%	(0.89)%	(4.11)%	
Average Profit/Loss:	0.48 %	3.73 %	(3.40)%	
Average SPX Profit/Loss:	0.35 %	0.80 %	(0.18)%	
Probability:		54.13 %	45.16 %	
Average Annual ROI:	24.35 %	187.07 %	(171.80)%	
Annual SPX (Buy & Hold):	14.34 %			
Reward/Risk Ratio:	1.32			
Start test date:	01/03/06			
End test date:	05/01/07			

Interval: Daily
Pricing Summary
Entry price: [Open]
Exit price: [Open]
Exit Summary
Hold for 5 periods

Courtesy of AIQ

FIGURE 2.5:
TRADE DATES FOR BASIC PATTERN BACKTEST
JAN. 2006 TO MAY 2007

Ticker	Held	Entry Date	Entry Price	Exit Date	Exit Price	Profit
PDCO	7	09/08/06	31.1200	09/15/06	31.7300	0.6100
DAKT	7	09/07/06	21.1300	09/14/06	20.3600	-0.7700
BJ	7	09/06/06	26.3300	09/13/06	27.8600	1.5300
HOTT	7	09/06/06	9.9900	09/13/06	10.5100	0.5200
FLWS	7	09/05/06	4.7500	09/12/06	5.1400	0.3900
ABI	10	09/01/06	30.9200	09/11/06	31.6000	0.6800
GPRO	10	09/01/06	48.6000	09/11/06	46.7000	-1.9000
ISLE	10	09/01/06	20.4100	09/11/06	21.1500	0.7400
OLN	10	09/01/06	15.1500	09/11/06	15.5800	0.4300
PLXS	10	09/01/06	19.8300	09/11/06	18.5900	-1.2400
SSD	10	09/01/06	26.3500	09/11/06	25.3200	-1.0300
GWR	8	08/31/06	24.2700	09/08/06	23.2300	-1.0400
MRCY	8	08/31/06	12.5100	09/08/06	11.9200	-0.5900
ADPT	8	08/29/06	3.9900	09/06/06	4.1600	0.1700
AIN	8	08/29/06	34.0900	09/06/06	35.5500	1.4600
AIR	8	08/29/06	21.0000	09/06/06	23.0000	2.0000
CEPH	8	08/29/06	58.5500	09/06/06	57.9900	-0.5600
CHH	8	08/29/06	37.4500	09/06/06	39.2300	1.7800
CRDN	8	08/29/06	42.1000	09/06/06	44.5400	2.4400
CYT	8	08/29/06	51.0000	09/06/06	53.8000	2.8000
EAGL	8	08/29/06	30.0900	09/06/06	30.8700	0.7800
GPN	8	08/29/06	37.5500	09/06/06	38.4700	0.9200
IMN	8	08/29/06	38.5000	09/06/06	39.8900	1.3900
LEE	8	08/29/06	24.2500	09/06/06	24.9700	0.7200
NI	8	08/29/06	21.1500	09/06/06	21.1000	-0.0500
RNT	8	08/29/06	22.7900	09/06/06	24.0000	1.2100
RYAAY	8	08/29/06	26.9800	09/06/06	28.8200	1.8400
SGMS	8	08/29/06	28.9800	09/06/06	29.0900	0.1100
TMA	8	08/29/06	23.2600	09/06/06	23.3600	0.1000
TNH	8	08/29/06	20.0500	09/06/06	21.6000	1.5500
TXI	8	08/29/06	46.2500	09/06/06	47.9500	1.7000
AOS	8	08/28/06	40.2000	09/05/06	40.6300	0.4300
CBG	8	08/28/06	21.4400	09/05/06	22.9500	1.5100
CECO	8	08/28/06	18.2200	09/05/06	19.7800	1.5600
CMOS	8	08/28/06	2.1300	09/05/06	2.6400	0.5100
CTB	8	08/28/06	8.5000	09/05/06	9.9300	1.4300
FINL	8	08/28/06	10.7300	09/05/06	11.4100	0.6800
GY	8	08/28/06	13.6700	09/05/06	14.0400	0.3700
JCOM	8	08/28/06	24.0300	09/05/06	25.1900	1.1600
KG	8	08/28/06	16.4200	09/05/06	16.3200	-0.1000

For Help, press F1   Items: 3087   NUM

Courtesy of AIQ

EXPANDED TEST PERIOD OF 16 MONTHS

Figure 2.4 shows the results of running the same test with the sole exception of changing the test period to the 16-month period from 01/03/06 to 05/01/07. This second test sheds some additional light on the bullish engulfing pattern. The number of trades increased from 691 to 3,087, which is by a factor of 4.46. The test period increased from 4 to 16 months, which is an increase of a factor of 4. This indicates that, on average, the bullish engulfing pattern is generating about the same number of trades per month in two different time periods. This is important to be sure that the pattern is producing consistent patterns and that they are not a function of some event that may or may not occur again.

Another way to check that a trading pattern is producing trades on a regular basis and not clustered around some event is to have the backtesting program show you a list of all the trades that were taken in the simulation and to simply sort them by date and scroll through the list looking for the regular occurrence of trades. This takes about a minute and an example of the list of specific trades taken for the second simulation is shown in Figure 2.5.

Figure 2.5 shows that bullish engulfing patterns occur regularly on most trading days, which is a good place to be when starting the evaluation of a trading pattern. If the trade dates came in groups or clusters with long

FIGURE 2.6:
NASDAQ DURING THE JANUARY '06 TO MAY '07 PERIOD

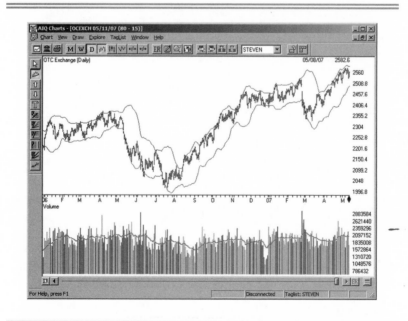

Courtesy of AIQ

time periods between them, it may indicate that the patterns were driven by occasional events rather than being a normal part of the trading process.

Looking back at the information in Figure 2.4, it is interesting to note that both the annualized ROI and the percentage of winning trades dropped when the bullish engulfing pattern was tested in the 16-month time frame as compared to the four-month time frame. The drop in both is fairly significant, indicating it is something worth further investigation. Analyzing a trading pattern through backtesting is a bit like a scavenger hunt; you cannot find the good stuff unless you look.

Figure 2.6 shows the market environment during the January 2006 to May 2007 test period that was used to gather the data shown in Figure 2.4. During this period, the market moved within a trading range during the first four months of 2006. It then dropped for three months, which was then followed by a nice bull run for four moths, and finally led to another three month trading range. During the first test period, the market was moving mostly up. In the longer test period, the market showed two sideways movements, one extended down move, and two up moves. Backtesting can be used to determine if these changes in market conditions affect the results of trading the bullish engulfing pattern.

DETERMINING THE EFFECT OF DIFFERENT MARKET CONDITIONS

Running the bullish engulfing pattern backtest from 07/21/06 to 05/01/07 removes the January 2006 to July 2006 period from the results and results in improvement in both the ROI and percentage of winning trades as compared to the previous January 2006 to May 2007 test period. Up to this point, we have run three backtests and found stronger ROI and winning percentage results during the test periods when the market was strong and less impressive results when the test period included periods of market sideways movement or drops.

Testing trading patterns in each of the three basic market environments—bullish, bearish, and trading range—allows us to know which trading patterns to use by just looking at a chart of the market. If the market is in a clear uptrend, then focus on the trading patterns that have tested well in uptrends. If the market is bearish, then use trading patterns that tested well in downtrends. And, of course, when the market moves in a trading range, trade the patterns that have tested well in this environment.

Predicting the Future

One of the more interesting observations about the market is that it usually does not look the same from year to year. The next year or two-year period usually does not look just like the last year or two-year period. The next five-year period usually does not look like the last five-year period. The implications of this observation are significant for backtesting and for developing trading tools. Projecting the future market behavior based on the last year or two is prone to failure. The market does not often repeat time periods, which makes predicting the future based on recent time periods difficult.

If backtesting results are based on past time periods, it makes it difficult to project them into the future. Yet, the market provides a way for traders to address this problem. Whatever it does in the future, the patterns will always be made out of a series of bull, bear, and trading range periods. The market can only go up, down, or sideways. Knowing this, we must figure out which patterns work in each of the three types of market conditions in order to be successful.

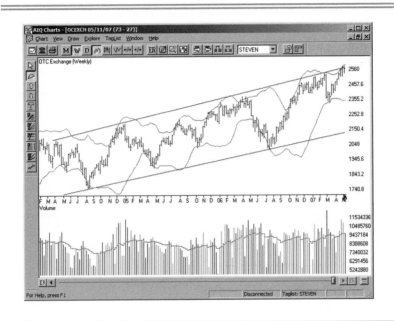

Courtesy of AIQ

TESTING AN ASCENDING CHANNEL

Figure 2.7 shows a chart of market activity between January 2004 and May 2007. During this time, the market was trading in an ascending channel and showed several clear up and down trends lasting for several months. Test results for trading the bullish engulfing pattern during this entire period, and just during the up and down trends within it, are shown in Table 2.2.

The results shown in Table 2.2 are striking. Trading the bullish engulfing pattern just during each of the two bull market moves yielded a significantly better ROI and better winning percentages than trading the pattern during the entire 01/16/04 to 05/01/07 period. Even more interesting is that trading the pattern during each of the two bear market environments during this period resulted in significantly lower annualized ROI and dropped the winning percentage of trades to under 50%.

TABLE 2.2.
TEST RESULTS FOR BULLISH ENGULFING PATTERN BETWEEN JAN. 2004 AND MAY 2007

	TEST PERIOD	ANNUALIZED ROI	WINNING PERCENTAGE
Full:	01/16/04 to 05/01/07	16%	52%
Bull:	08/13/04 to 12/31/04	122%	69%
Bull:	07/28/06 to 11/24/06	46%	55%
Bear:	12/31/04 to 04/29/05	<48%>	40%
Bear:	05/05/06 to 07/21/06	3%	49%

Market Adaptive Trading

This kind of test data is one of the reasons I trade using a process of market adaptive trading (MAT). Different market environments favor different types of trading patterns and exit strategies. After carefully testing a variety of trading patterns in each of the three different market conditions, it becomes clear which patterns are the most appropriate to be using in the current environment. Additional information on market adaptive trading techniques may be found in the last chapter and online at www.daisydogger.com. Remember, the market will not adapt to us, so we must adapt to it.

VARYING THE HOLDING PERIOD

The market conditions have a clear effect on the results when trading the bullish engulfing pattern. The next parameter to investigate is the holding period. On all of the tests so far, we have entered a trade at the market open the day after a bullish engulfing pattern forms and then held the position for five days, exiting on the opening value after the fifth day. The fewer arbitrary things in trading the better; so, Table 2.3 shows the results of running the bullish engulfing test pattern between 01/03/06 and 05/01/07 (the same test period used for the results shown in Figure 2.4) and varying only the holding period. The results for the five day holding period are the same as shown in Figure 2.4.

Good try — rigid rules!

The results of Table 2.3 indicate that holding periods between five and seven days produce similar results. The performance of the bullish engulfing pattern declines with holding periods shorter than five days or longer than seven days. It is like visiting the in-laws and either not staying long enough to see every one, or staying too long and wearing out your welcome. Trading patterns, like visits, have an optimum stay. *This is truly a surprise!*

TABLE 2.3.
TEST RESULTS FOR JANUARY 2004 AND
MAY 2007 WITH DIFFERENT HOLDING PERIODS

HOLDING PERIOD	ANNUALIZED ROI	WINNING PERCENTAGE
3 Days	13%	51%
4	16%	53%
5	24%	54%
6	26%	55%
7	24%	55%
8	20%	55%
9	19%	55%
15	14%	53%

+ technique lost a lot by not exiting when + market suggested + it says nothing of stop losses.

TESTING STOCK PRICE LEVEL

Some traders like to trade low dollar stocks because they feel there is more bang for the buck. Other traders like to trade large dollar stocks because they feel they "behave better." One of the keys to trading is to focus on trades and filters that will produce data indicating that your idea has a real effect on the results. The market does not care what we think or feel. Trading by feeling is eventually going to lead to trouble. Testing and analyzing a pattern yields insight into what type of filters really matter. Doing the analysis also builds confidence and makes it easier to trade with less emotion.

Table 2.4 shows the results of testing the bullish engulfing pattern during the January 2006 to May 2007 time period, with the same five day holding period we have used in the previous tests. The difference is that a filter has been added to eliminate stocks in the database below a certain price level. This allows us to determine if the price level of the stock would have made a difference for trading during this period.

TABLE 2.4.
TEST RESULTS FOR JANUARY 2006 TO
MAY 2007 WITH DIFFERENT PRICE LEVELS

PRICE LEVEL FILTER	ANNUALIZED ROI	WINNING PERCENTAGE
None	24%	54%
Stock > $10	21%	54%
Stock > $20	22%	55%
Stock > $30	20%	55%
Stock > $50	17%	55%
Stock > $70	14%	54%

The results shown in Table 2.4 indicate that the percentage of winning trades for bullish engulfing patterns is about the same during the test period regardless of the dollar value of the stocks. It also shows that the annualized ROI tends to drop slightly as the trading price of the stock increases. The results are not striking enough to cause us to focus only on trading bullish engulfing patterns in low dollar stocks; but, if I had several patterns to choose from and only room in my trading portfolio for one more position, I would look at price as one of the factors for selecting the trade.

USING AN AVERAGE VOLUME FILTER

Deciding whether to take a trade and which trade to pick if there are several choices available should be based on the preponderance of evidence. A jury may not acquit because of one specific fact; but, if several facts indicate the possibility of innocence or guilt, the jurors would make a decision based on the preponderance of evidence. Trading is similar. It is rare that everything lines up perfectly, and there is often some contradictory evidence. The trader must carefully analyze a trading pattern and then make a decision based on what most of the evidence is indicating.

Note that, unlike a jury, a trader does not have the ability to deliberate for a week or two before making a decision. Trading patterns are perishable; they have a shelf life. Traders need to have well-researched patterns and a clear understanding of the effects of various trading parameters to quickly make a decision and move on to the next issue. Some factors, like whether the market is bullish or bearish, have a strong impact on results, as we have seen from the previous tests. Other factors, like the price of the stock being traded, are relatively minor influences. In order to last in the trading business, it is important to know which factors have a significant impact on results, and which ones are second-order issues.

Table 2.5 shows the results of testing the bullish engulfing pattern in the January 2006 to May 2007 time period using an average volume filter. The average volume filter eliminated stocks whose 21 day simple average volume was less than the amounts shown in Table 2.5. The first line shows the test results for the period using no average volume filter, and they are the same as shown previously. The second line shows the results for only taking bullish engulfing trades during the test period when the average volume was at least 300,000 shares a day.

The data in Table 2.5 is interesting and indicates that, for this test period, bullish engulfing patterns perform better when trading stocks whose average daily volume is below a million shares a day. There are a lot of stocks in this category, so there are plenty of trades to take if traders add this filter to the pattern.

TABLE 2.5.
TEST RESULTS FOR JANUARY 2006 TO
MAY 2007 WITH DIFFERENT VOLUME LEVELS

VOLUME LEVEL FILTER	ANNUALIZED ROI	WINNING PERCENTAGE
None	24%	54%
Average Volume > 300,000	23%	54%
Average Volume > 600,000	17%	54%
Average Volume > 1,000,000	18%	53%
Average Volume > 2,000,000	10%	52%
Average Volume > 3,000,000	7%	51%
Average Volume > 4,000,000	10%	51%

At this point you may be wondering, "Why is the annualized ROI better for stocks with average daily volume under a million shares?" A lot of reasons can be offered, but when trading patterns we focus on what works. We are not trading the explanation; we are trading the pattern that has shown interesting results over thousands of trades.

Traders want to gather as much useful information about their tools as possible like a car owner who wants to know how far the car can go on a tank of gas, how often the oil should be changed, how much weight the car can tow, how to use the air conditioner and lights, etc. This knowledge helps get the best use from the car and allows it to be used in different conditions—hot or cold, day or night. Similarly, the trader needs to know how price, volume, and market conditions affect the results of using trading patterns to get the best use from them.

↑ trend
hold 5-7 days
Avg Vol < 1 M shares

TESTING FIRST DAY VERSUS SECOND DAY VOLUME

So far we have seen that the bullish engulfing pattern performs significantly better when the market is trending up than when it is trending down. It tends to perform better with holding periods between five and seven days, and results are improved when trading stocks whose average volume is under one million shares a day. As we continue investigating the pattern, we will find other characteristics and parameters that help us use the pattern more effectively.

The premise behind the bullish engulfing pattern is that the first day is a black-bodied candlestick representing a down day (a continuation of the stocks downtrend), and the second day of the pattern is a white body that covers or engulfs the previous day's black body, indicating that the downtrend may be over. If volume indicates the level interest in a move, then would the pattern show better results if the second day's white engulfing body occurred on larger volume than the previous day's volume?

Figure 2.8 shows the testing results for the basic bullish engulfing pattern with the standard five day holding period with one additional filter that

FIGURE 2.8:
TESTING INCREASED SECOND DAY VOLUME DURING JAN. 2006 TO MAY 2007

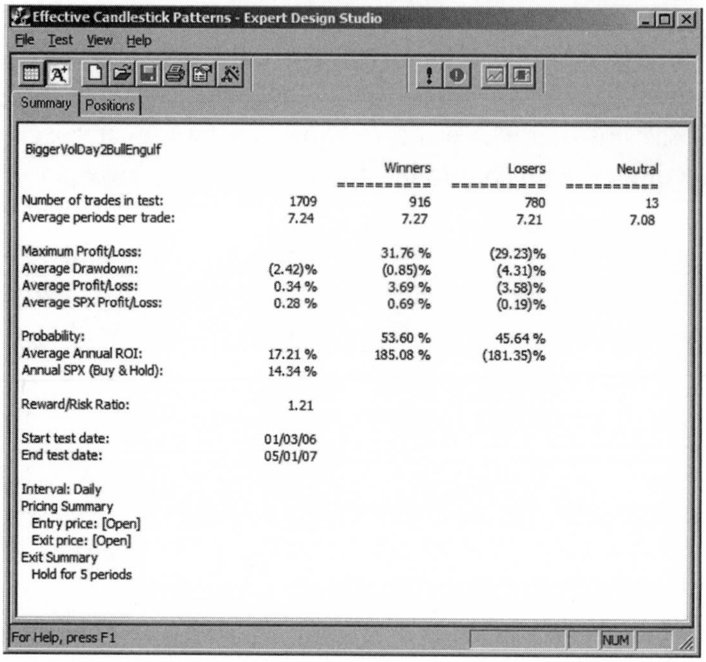

BiggerVolDay2BullEngulf

		Winners	Losers	Neutral
Number of trades in test:	1709	916	780	13
Average periods per trade:	7.24	7.27	7.21	7.08
Maximum Profit/Loss:		31.76 %	(29.23)%	
Average Drawdown:	(2.42)%	(0.85)%	(4.31)%	
Average Profit/Loss:	0.34 %	3.69 %	(3.58)%	
Average SPX Profit/Loss:	0.28 %	0.69 %	(0.19)%	
Probability:		53.60 %	45.64 %	
Average Annual ROI:	17.21 %	185.08 %	(181.35)%	
Annual SPX (Buy & Hold):	14.34 %			
Reward/Risk Ratio:	1.21			
Start test date:	01/03/06			
End test date:	05/01/07			

Interval: Daily
Pricing Summary
Entry price: [Open]
Exit price: [Open]
Exit Summary
Hold for 5 periods

Courtesy of AIQ

requires the volume on the second day of the pattern to be larger than the volume on the first day. With the exception of the new volume filter, the test is the same as that used to produce the data in Figure 2.4.

It is interesting to note that adding a requirement to the basic bullish engulfing pattern that the volume on the second day of the pattern be larger than the volume on the first day actually reduced the annualized ROI. Running the test again with the requirement that the second day's volume be at least 120% of the first day's volume decreased the annualized ROI to 11%. A third run with the requirement that the volume on the second day of the bullish engulfing pattern be at least 140% of the volume on the first day of the pattern further reduced the annualized ROI to 9% and dropped the percentage of winning trades during this test period to 52%.

Looking for stronger volume on the second day of the bullish engulfing pattern seems quite logical. The advantage of testing these assumptions is that, like words from a politician, things are not always what they seem. Testing does not guarantee a future result; there are no guarantees in trading. If you want a guarantee, buy a tool from Sears. Testing does however provide insight into trading patterns and gives traders an understanding of what has been effective over thousands of previous trades.

If instead of looking for strong volume on the second day of the pattern, we look for strong volume on the first day of the two day pattern, will the results improve? When testing the basic bullish engulfing pattern during the period of January 2006 to May of 2007 and adding a filter to take trades in stocks only when the volume on the first day of the pattern was at least 110% of the 21 day simple average of the volume, the annualized ROI increased to 33% and the percentage of winning trades was 56%.

The above average volume on the down day of the pattern may indicate that most of those interested in selling in the short run have done so, thus on the second day, when the stock bounces and engulfs the previous day's black body, the bulls have control.

EXAMINING KEY MOVING AVERAGES

Many traders use moving averages as one way of determining if stocks are overbought or oversold. The 50 and 200 period moving averages are two of the more common ones that are watched. Some mutual funds will not purchase stocks below their 200 day averages and some traders believe that stocks trading above their 50 day moving averages are basically strong. Given this information, it is reasonable to look at whether the results of trading the bullish engulfing pattern in stocks above or below key moving averages makes a difference in results.

Figure 2.9 shows the results of testing the bullish engulfing pattern with the requirement that trades are only taken in stocks that are below their 50 day simple moving average during the period of January 2006 to May of 2007. The results are not significantly different than those obtained without this requirement. From this data, it appears that using the 50 period moving average is not an effective filter.

What if instead of only taking bullish engulfing trades when the stock is below its 50 period moving average, we take trades only when the stock is below its seven period moving average. We find the results are quite different. In this case the annualized ROI increases from 24% to 31% and the percentage of winning trades increases to 56%.

For a stock to be above the seven period moving average, it must have been moving sideways to up for a short period of time. Since the basic bullish engulfing test looks for stocks in a downtrend, this implies that candidate stocks have been moving down but then moved sideways or up for a brief period. An example of this behavior is shown in Figure 2.10, where ABAX

FIGURE 2.9:
TESTING BULLISH ENGULFING BELOW 50 MA DURING JANUARY '06 TO MAY '07

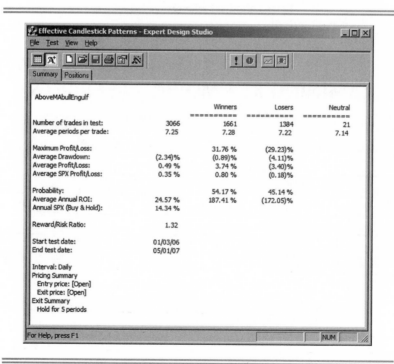

Courtesy of AIQ

formed a bullish engulfing pattern on 11/08/06 after a brief bounce or retrace of the overall downtrend.

Filtering out stocks with this behavior by using the seven period moving average improves results. This indicates that perhaps results could be improved further by finding candidates that have not bounced or retraced during their downtrend. Since this is the case, let's continue our research.

Testing the standard bullish engulfing pattern over the period of January 2006 to May 2007 with the additional requirement that the first day of the pattern (the black body day) have the lowest low in the previous five days improved the annualized ROI to 26% and the percentage of winning trades increased to 56%. The results are interesting but not dramatic.

FIGURE 2.10:
ABAX BULLISH ENGULFING ON 11/08/06 AFTER A BRIEF BOUNCE

Courtesy of AIQ

INVESTIGATING BODIES AND SHADOWS

We investigated whether the size of the first day's black body in relationship to the overall trading range for the day had an impact on results. Testing for small first day black body sizes, less than 80% of the total day's trading range, showed little impact on trading results. It is interesting, though, that only taking trades when the first day's black body was at least 80% of the day's trading range reduced both the annualized ROI and the percentage of winning trades. This indicates that when there is a choice, the trader should pass on patterns where the first day is a large black body with little or no shadows.

FIGURE 2.11:
LARGE UPPER SHADOW IN CMG
BULLISH ENGULFING ON 07/28/06

Courtesy of AIQ

Figure 2.11 shows an example of a bullish engulfing pattern that occurred in CMG on 07/28/06 where the first day (as marked by the up arrow) had a large upper shadow. The data in Table 2.6 indicates that as the upper shadow of the pattern increases in size to about 50% of the daily range, the annualized ROI increases significantly and the percentage of winning trades remains about the same.

The increase in annualized ROI is attributable to the fact that the winning trades gain more and the losing trades lose less as the size of the upper shadow is increased. The average trade gains more but the percentage of winning trades remains about the same.

TABLE 2.6
TEST RESULTS FOR 01/03/06 TO 05/01/07 WITH
DIFFERENT DAY 1 UPPER SHADOW LENGTHS

UPPER SHADOW AS % OF DAY'S RANGE	ANNUALIZED ROI	WINNING PERCENTAGE
No Requirement	24%	54%
Shadow > 10% of Day's Range	28%	54%
Shadow > 20% of Day's Range	31%	55%
Shadow > 30% of Day's Range	34%	56%
Shadow > 40% of Day's Range	38%	56%
Shadow > 50% of Day's Range	41%	56%
Shadow > 60% of Day's Range	27%	53%

Table 2.7 shows the results of testing the effect of the size of the lower shadow on the second day of the bullish engulfing pattern. Long lower shadows indicate that after the open, the stock's price was driven down, but then later rallied to close up for the day. This is consistent with the idea that the second day of the pattern is a reversal in sentiment.

The results are interesting, and they indicate that longer lower shadows on the second day of the pattern increase the annualized ROI up to the point where the lower shadow is about 30% of the day's trading range. When the lower shadow on the second day of the bullish engulfing pattern exceeds 30% of the day's range, the results become inconsistent.

TABLE 2.7
TEST RESULTS FOR 01/03/06 TO 05/01/07 WITH DIFFERENT DAY 2 LOWER SHADOW LENGTHS

LOWER SHADOW AS % OF DAY'S RANGE	ANNUALIZED ROI	WINNING PERCENTAGE
No Requirement	24%	54%
Shadow > 10% of Day's Range	34%	55%
Shadow > 20% of Day's Range	38%	55%
Shadow > 30% of Day's Range	41%	58%
Shadow > 40% of Day's Range	26%	57%
Shadow > 50% of Day's Range	37%	56%

An example of a long-tailed second day bullish engulfing pattern is shown in Figure 2.12 for DRIV. The long lower shadow on the second day's white body is the type of filter that was added to produce the results in Table 2.7.

We have looked at testing data for the basic bullish engulfing pattern in different market conditions as well as for different price and volume characteristics of the candidate stocks. We have also investigated the effects of varying the body and shadow sizes of the pattern itself. There are other parameters that can be investigated, but at some point we have to conclude the testing of various parameters and look at the results of combining filters, verifying results in different time periods, and managing the trade.

FIGURE 2.12:

LONG LOWER SHADOW IN DRIV BULLISH ENGULFING ON 02/07/07

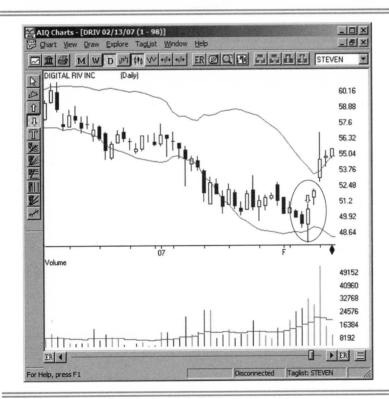

Courtesy of AIQ

MANAGING THE EXIT

The test results so far have indicated the bullish engulfing pattern works considerably better in uptrending markets than during periods when the market is in a downtrend, and that the pattern typically takes a few days to work, with holding times between four and seven days being best. Exit strategies are a key part of trading. I rarely enter a position without knowing where I will exit, both in terms of a profit target if the trade goes well, and a stop loss in case the trade moves against me.

Why does he/lot + mkt tell him?

After entering a trade, I enter a stop loss just under a recent low. This initial stop loss protects the account from serious damage if something goes wrong. The logic behind selecting a recent low for a stop loss is that the bullish engulfing pattern is supposed to mark the end of a downtrend in the stock. If the stock undercuts a recent low, then by definition the downtrend has not ended and it is best to move on to another trade.

Figure 2.13 shows a bullish engulfing pattern in Y that occurred on 01/20/06 and is marked by the down arrow. The trading process would be to enter a long position at the next day's opening price and hold for five days, which would result in a profitable trade. The recent low in Y happened two day's prior to the pattern formation and was the low of the day on 01/18/06. A stop loss order entered just under the low of 01/18/06, as noted by the horizontal line in Figure 2.13, would be triggered if Y moved down and undercut this previous low.

Remember, that a downtrend is defined as a stock making a series of lower lows and lower highs. If Y were to make a lower low after the occurrence of the bullish engulfing pattern, it would be an indication that the pattern did not mark the end of the downtrend and, therefore, losses should be cut short and capital moved into another trade. It is usually a bad idea to hold on and hope that things will get better. Trade the patterns, not your hopes. We hope every trade is profitable, but experience and backtesting tell us that is not the case. Remember when the chart shows that the pattern has not done what it is supposed to do, it is time to cut losses and move to another trade.

Some traders like to enter stops based on a percentage like 5% or 7% of the entry price. It is a common practice, and may be better than not having a

Courtesy of AIQ

stop. However, when trading chart patterns, the pattern itself is what got us into the trade, and the failure of the pattern, or reaching a target price or time interval, should be what gets us out of the trade.

HOW TO AVOID
CURVE FITTING: EXTENDED TESTING

A common suggestion by traders new to backtesting is to just combine all the filters that improve results and trade the resulting system. Sometimes it works and sometimes it does not. Just like everything else, the results of combining filters need to be tested. It is possible to keep adding filters to a trading pattern until most of the losing trades in a given time period have been filtered out. This is called curve fitting.

In order to make sure we are not just curve fitting the data during one test period, we need to verify that the different filters work in more than one time period. We also must verify that there are enough trades remaining after adding the filters for the resulting tests to be statistically significant. If one had two trading systems that produced the same annualized ROI and percentage of winning trades during the same period, one might expect them to be equivalent. However, like most mathematical things, there is more to the story.

If one trading system produced 10 trades a year and another produced 200 trades a year, it is more likely that the second system could be expected to repeat in the future. A larger number of trades make it less likely that one or two big trades are strongly influencing the average result. Each of the tests run above resulted in a very large number of trades. As we add more than one filter, the number of trades during the test period will be reduced, and we need to make sure there are still enough trades for the results to be meaningful.

Figure 2.14 shows the results of extending the test period for the basic bullish engulfing pattern by two years to include trading all basic bullish engulfing patterns found between January 2004 and May 2007. This extended period shows a drop in the annualized ROI from 24% when testing in the January 2006 to May 2007 period, to 16% annualized ROI for the January 2004 to May 2007 period. The percentage of winning trades dropped slightly from 54% in the shorter test period to 52% in the longer test.

Doubling the test period includes the results of more than twice as many trades and yet the percentage of winning trades is nearly the same. This indicates that the percentage of winners is roughly the same in multiple time periods, and the results are most likely due to the nature of the pattern itself and not the specific time frame in which the testing was done.

Our previous research indicated that market conditions are a factor in the results of using this pattern. Figure 2.15 shows the test results for the new extended period (January 2004 to May 2007) with the addition of a filter that only takes trades when the NASDAQ is in an uptrend. The NASDAQ is determined to be in an uptrend if the highest value in the last six sessions is greater than the highest price of the stock in the previous 30 sessions.

When the uptrend filter is added to the basic bullish engulfing pattern, the results improved significantly, the annualized ROI more than doubled, and the percentage of winning trades increased. This verifies the previous results that bullish market conditions improve the results of trading the pattern. As a practical matter, traders can either incorporate the NASDAQ uptrend filter into scans for the bullish engulfing pattern, or simply use trend lines drawn on the NASDAQ to determine when to take bullish engulfing pattern trades.

FIGURE 2.14:
BASIC BULLISH ENGULFING TEST
BETWEEN JAN. '04 AND MAY '07

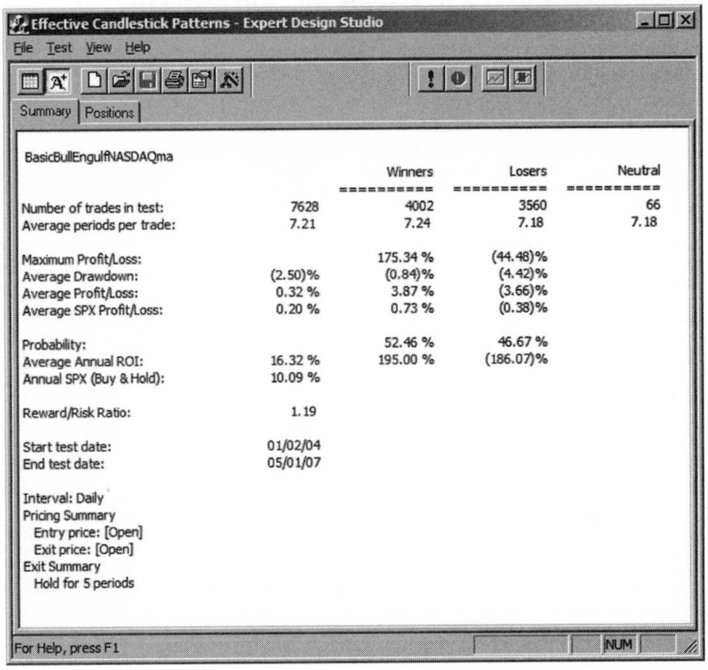

Effective Candlestick Patterns - Expert Design Studio				_ □ x

File Test View Help

Summary | Positions |

BasicBullEngulfNASDAQma

		Winners	Losers	Neutral
Number of trades in test:	7628	4002	3560	66
Average periods per trade:	7.21	7.24	7.18	7.18
Maximum Profit/Loss:		175.34 %	(44.48)%	
Average Drawdown:	(2.50)%	(0.84)%	(4.42)%	
Average Profit/Loss:	0.32 %	3.87 %	(3.66)%	
Average SPX Profit/Loss:	0.20 %	0.73 %	(0.38)%	
Probability:		52.46 %	46.67 %	
Average Annual ROI:	16.32 %	195.00 %	(186.07)%	
Annual SPX (Buy & Hold):	10.09 %			
Reward/Risk Ratio:	1.19			
Start test date:	01/02/04			
End test date:	05/01/07			

Interval: Daily
Pricing Summary
  Entry price: [Open]
  Exit price: [Open]
Exit Summary
  Hold for 5 periods

For Help, press F1 — NUM

Courtesy of AIQ

Adding both a NASDAQ uptrend filter and a filter requiring the average daily volume be less than one million shares results in a lower annualized ROI and winning trade percentage during the extended test period. The volume filter looked promising in initial tests, but did not hold up on further examination. Traders should not base trades on the results of just one or two tests. Filters that appear to help should always be tested in different time periods and market conditions to see if the result is an effective addition to the pattern, or just something related to a particular time period.

Backtesting the bullish engulfing pattern during the January 2004 to May 2007 period and using both the NASDAQ uptrend filter and the requirement that the first day of the pattern occur on above average volume increased the annualized ROI to 46% and also increased the percentage of winning trades

FIGURE 2.15:
BASIC BULLISH ENGULFING TEST WITH NASDAQ UPTREND FILTER BETWEEN JAN. '04 AND MAY '07

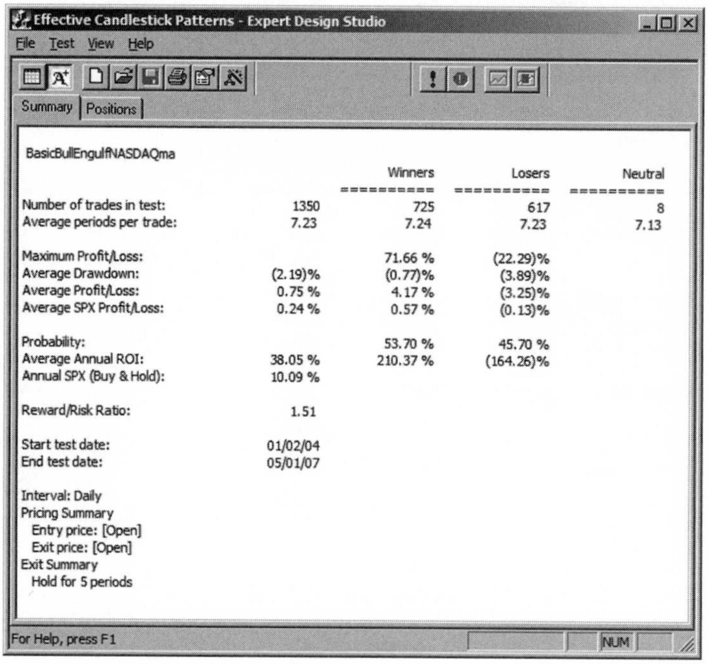

Courtesy of AIQ

to 55%. These two filters work well together and significantly improve the results of trading the bullish engulfing pattern.

Using filters for the NASDAQ being in an uptrend and also a large upper shadow on the first day of the pattern did not significantly improve results over those shown in Figure 2.15. The filter for a long lower shadow on the second day of the pattern also improved results over the basic bullish engulfing pattern, but not as much as either the uptrend filter for the NASDAQ or the filter for large volume on the first day of the pattern. The filters for requiring the NASDAQ to be in an uptrend and requiring above average volume on the first day of the pattern yielded strong enough results. The other filters just reduced the number of trades without further increasing annualized ROI and the percentage of winning trades.

FIGURE 2.16:
BULLISH ENGULFING WITH UPTRENDING NASDAQ AND
LARGE VOLUME FIRST DAY BETWEEN JANUARY '04 AND MAY '07

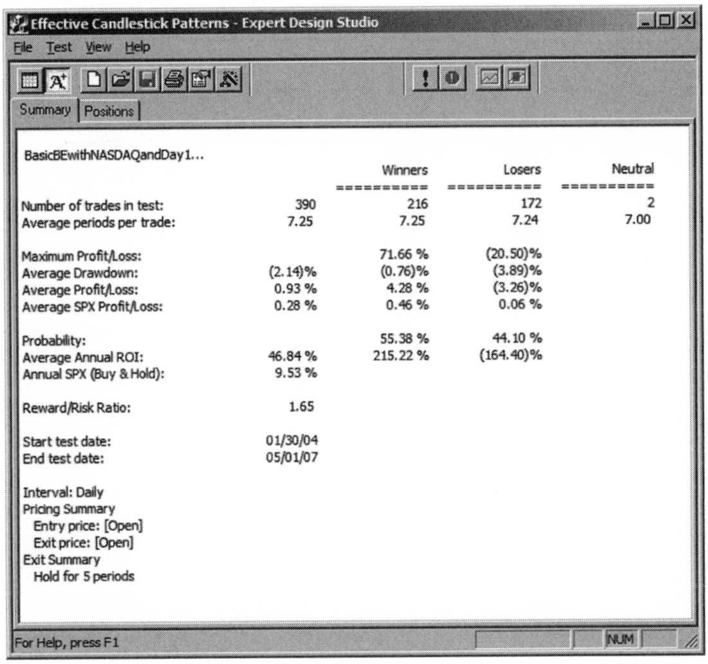

Effective Candlestick Patterns - Expert Design Studio			
File Test View Help			

BasicBEwithNASDAQandDay1...		Winners	Losers	Neutral
Number of trades in test:	390	216	172	2
Average periods per trade:	7.25	7.25	7.24	7.00
Maximum Profit/Loss:		71.66 %	(20.50)%	
Average Drawdown:	(2.14)%	(0.76)%	(3.89)%	
Average Profit/Loss:	0.93 %	4.28 %	(3.26)%	
Average SPX Profit/Loss:	0.28 %	0.46 %	0.06 %	
Probability:		55.38 %	44.10 %	
Average Annual ROI:	46.84 %	215.22 %	(164.40)%	
Annual SPX (Buy & Hold):	9.53 %			
Reward/Risk Ratio:	1.65			
Start test date:	01/30/04			
End test date:	05/01/07			
Interval: Daily				
Pricing Summary				
Entry price: [Open]				
Exit price: [Open]				
Exit Summary				
Hold for 5 periods				

For Help, press F1 — NUM

Courtesy of AIQ

It is very interesting that adding two simple filters to the basic bullish engulfing pattern nearly triples the annualized ROI and also increases the percentage of winning trades. Figure 2.16 shows the results of backtesting the bullish engulfing pattern during the January 2004 to May 2007 period with the additional requirements that the NASDAQ is uptrending and the first day of the pattern is occuring on above average volume. Backtesting takes some time and effort, but it leads to a better understanding of what to expect from a trading pattern. In this case, it also led to two simple additions to the pattern that nearly tripled the trading results.

FINAL RESULTS—HOW TO TRADE THE BULLISH ENGULFING

The backtesting indicates that the results of using the bullish engulfing patterns are improved by:

- Trading the pattern when the market is in an uptrend.
- Trading stocks with average daily volume less than one million shares.
- Looking for above average volume on day one of the pattern.
- Trading stocks below their seven day simple moving average.
- Looking for large upper shadows on day one of the pattern.
- Looking for long lower shadows on day two of the pattern.

The backtesting also indicates that the trading results are not improved by:

- Limiting the price of the stock.
- Large volume on day two of the pattern.
- Trading stocks below their 50 day simple moving average.
- Requiring day one of the pattern to be the lowest low in the last 10 sessions.
- Requiring day one to have a small black body.

In summary, the bullish engulfing pattern is one that shows positive results in multiple time frames. After examining thousands of trades in multiple market conditions—and with a variety of different filters—we have seen that two simple additional requirements to the basic bullish engulfing pattern significantly improved the results. This trading pattern should be avoided when the market is in a downtrend. Knowing when not to use something is sometimes the most valuable information. Money not lost spends just as well as money made.

The trading results for the bullish engulfing pattern can also be significantly improved by focusing on trading patterns that have above average volume on the first day of this two day pattern. The effort put into backtesting allowed us to quickly analyze the results of thousands of trades and find two simple techniques to nearly triple the annualized ROI for this pattern.

The improved bullish engulfing pattern requirements are:

- The stock must be in a downtrend.
- The NASDAQ must be in an uptrend.
- The first day of the pattern must be a black-bodied candlestick that occurs on above average volume.
- The second day of the pattern must be a white-bodied candlestick whose body engulfs or overlaps the first day's body.
- Holding times should be between five and seven days.

┤CHAPTER 3├

BEARISH ENGULFING PATTERNS

One of the most common questions I get from subscribers to my newsletter, *The Timely Trades Letter,* usually comes from new subscribers who wonder how I "knew" that a recent setup would trigger and be profitable. New traders tend to believe there is a magic indicator that will tell them when a trade is going to work. This is not the case; there are no foolproof indicators that work all the time. Trading is about finding patterns that have favorable statistics, understanding how market conditions and various parameters affect the statistics, and then trading the pattern using effective money management techniques.

As we've seen, in order to better understand the statistics for a trading pattern, it can be backtested. Backtesting is not a guarantee of future results; it simply provides the trader with a good understanding of how the trading pattern has worked in the past. To build confidence that a trading pattern's results are likely to be replicated in the future, traders test them over hundreds or thousands of cases. It is a reasonable bet that something that has worked hundreds of times in the past has a reasonable chance of working in similar conditions in the future.

Remember, it is also important to test a potential trading pattern in multiple time frames and in different market conditions to gain a better idea of its overall performance and the type of market conditions in which it works best. You need to backtest potential trading patterns because not every pattern tests well in the long run. Knowing what not to trade may be just as important as knowing what to trade.

DEFINITION OF BEARISH ENGULFING PATTERN

Let's take a closer look at the bearish engulfing pattern. A bearish engulfing pattern may occur after a stock has been in an uptrend. The first day of this two day pattern shows a white body indicating that the stock was still moving up. The second day of the pattern has a black body that completely covers or engulfs the body of the previous day. The top of the black body represents the opening price, which has gapped up, and it is above the top of the previous day's body, which represents the closing price for the first day of the pattern. After the open on the second day, the stock may move up further, depending on whether the second day's candlestick has a top shadow or tail. Because the second day is a black candle, at some point during the day, the sentiment reversed and the price started declining. This may signal a further decline in the short term.

Figure 3.1 shows a bearish engulfing pattern that occurred in CEM on 04/17/07. CEM was trending up during March and the first half of April. On April 16, CEM showed a white bar followed by a black bar on the following day that overlapped or engulfed the white body of 04/16. The second day of the bearish engulfing pattern is marked by a down arrow in Figure 3.1. After the bearish engulfing pattern occurred, CEM moved down more than 4% in the next five days, creating a profitable short position.

If the bearish engulfing pattern marked the end of an uptrend and moved down every time it occurred, traders would quickly become rich by entering short positions when they observed bearish engulfing patterns forming. Unfortunately in actual practice, bearish engulfing patterns, like most trading patterns, have varying degrees of success. Some of the patterns work quite well, others generate small returns, and some lose. One of the tricks to

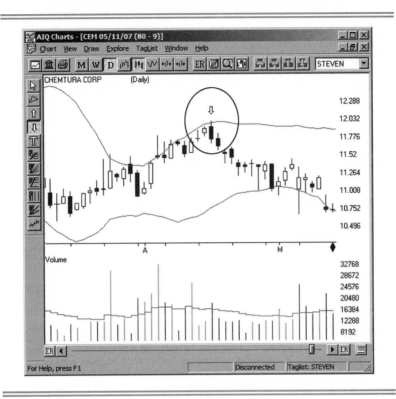

Courtesy of AIQ

trading patterns is to understand the factors that maximize the probability of a profitable trade.

Figure 3.2 shows a bearish engulfing pattern that occurred in DO on the same date, 04/17/07. In this case the bearish engulfing pattern, marked by the down arrow, did not mark the beginning of a significant change in trend as did the bearish engulfing pattern for CEM on the same date. Shorting DO resulted in a profitable trade for the first three days, followed by two days where the trade would have been about break even, followed by a resumption of the original uptrend, which would have resulted in a loss if the short position was held too long.

Figure 3.3 shows a third example of a bearish engulfing pattern that occurred on the same date, 04/17/07. GGB formed a bearish engulfing pattern on

FIGURE 3.2:
BEARISH ENGULFING PATTERN IN DO ON 4/17/07

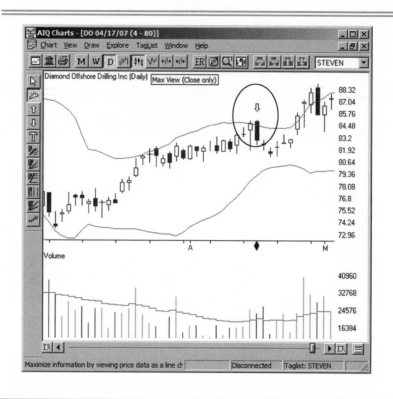

Courtesy of AIQ

04/17/07 as marked by the down arrow. In this case, the stock continued moving up over the next two weeks and a short position held for anywhere between one and 10 days would have been unprofitable.

DETERMINING THE OPTIMAL MARKET TO TRADE

The three bearish engulfing patterns I just outlined all occurred on the same date and yet provided different results for short positions. Like I've said before, trading is a statistical business and not every pattern results in a profitable trade. The trader must understand how often the pattern produces a profitable result and the effects of various parameters such as volume, price level, and average volume, as well as the effects of varying

Courtesy of AIQ

different parameters involved in the definition of the pattern. Bottom line, it's time to start testing again.

FIRST TEST PERIOD: 1/3/06 TO 5/1/07

Figure 3.4 shows the results of testing the bearish engulfing pattern during the period of 01/03/06 to 05/01/07. The results show that during this period the pattern not only performed worse than buy and hold, it actually lost money. In fact, losing trades occurred more than 55% of the time and less than 44% of the trades during this period resulted in a profit. The initial backtesting results raise a caution flag.

FIGURE 3.4:
BEARISH ENGULFING BACKTEST DURING 1/03/06 TO 5/01/07

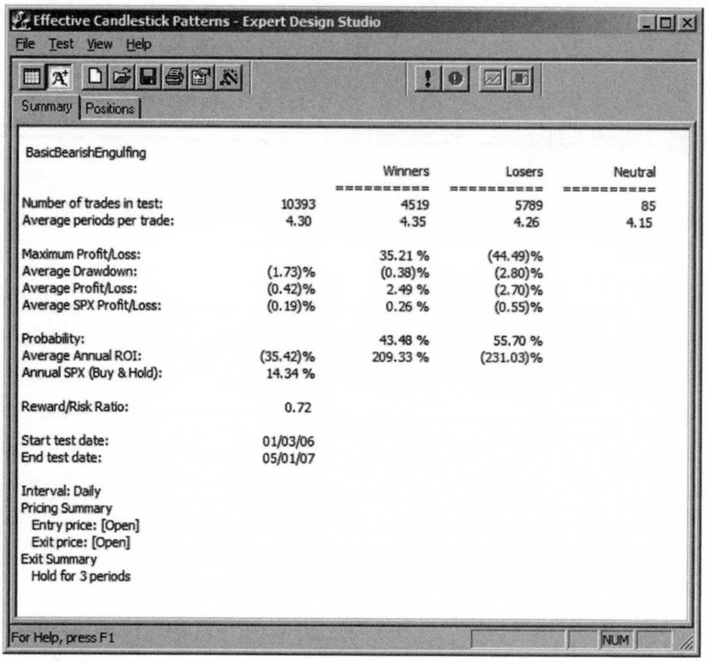

BasicBearishEngulfing

		Winners	Losers	Neutral
Number of trades in test:	10393	4519	5789	85
Average periods per trade:	4.30	4.35	4.26	4.15
Maximum Profit/Loss:		35.21 %	(44.49)%	
Average Drawdown:	(1.73)%	(0.38)%	(2.80)%	
Average Profit/Loss:	(0.42)%	2.49 %	(2.70)%	
Average SPX Profit/Loss:	(0.19)%	0.26 %	(0.55)%	
Probability:		43.48 %	55.70 %	
Average Annual ROI:	(35.42)%	209.33 %	(231.03)%	
Annual SPX (Buy & Hold):	14.34 %			
Reward/Risk Ratio:	0.72			
Start test date:	01/03/06			
End test date:	05/01/07			

Interval: Daily
Pricing Summary
Entry price: [Open]
Exit price: [Open]
Exit Summary
Hold for 3 periods

Courtesy of AIQ

TEST PERIOD INCREASED TO ONE YEAR

The market is always changing, and during certain market conditions some systems perform better than others. It is important to check a potential trading system in multiple time frames and also in different market conditions. Figure 3.5 shows the results of increasing the test period by a year and testing the basic bearish engulfing pattern during the period of 01/03/05 to 05/01/07.

Increasing the length of the testing period by one year significantly changed the results. The bearish engulfing pattern still shows a loss for the test period, but it was reduced from a loss of 35% for the first test to a smaller loss of 26% when adding a year to the test period. One possible explanation for this is that the results of using the bearish engulfing pattern depend on the market conditions in which it is used.

BEARISH ENGULFING BACKTEST DURING 1/03/05 TO 5/01/07

Courtesy of AIQ

In order to test this theory, we have to consider what different types of trading environments the market can present us with. We know there are only three things the market can do. It can move down, move up, or move mostly sideways. Testing the bearish engulfing pattern in each of these three different market conditions will let us know if the pattern works better in one of the three market types.

DOWNTREND MARKET

During the period of 12/31/04 to 04/28/05, the market was in a downtrend and dropped about 200 points, or about 10%, as shown in Figure 3.6. Testing the basic bearish engulfing pattern with a three day holding period during

FIGURE 3.6:
DECLINING MARKET DURING FIRST FOUR MONTHS OF 2005

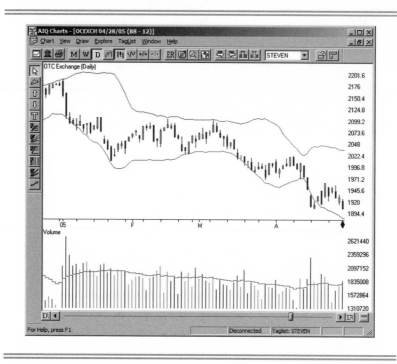

Courtesy of AIQ

this period resulted in 1,859 trades and a 31% annualized ROI, which is quite favorable as compared to the approximate 10% loss in the NASDAQ. Profitable trades equaled about 58% and only 40% resulted in losses. This is a significant improvement over the previous results.

SIDEWAYS MARKET

During the period of 11/17/05 to 03/13/06, the market moved mostly sideways within a 100 point range, as shown in Figure 3.7. Testing the basic bearish engulfing pattern during this period, when the market was stuck in a trading range, resulted in 2,880 trades and a 45% loss. Fewer than 45% of the trades were winners and more than 54% were losers. It would appear that at least in these two cases, the basic bearish engulfing pattern performs better when the market is in a downtrend than when it is moving sideways in a range.

FIGURE 3.7:
TRADING RANGE MARKET DURING
DECEMBER TO MARCH OF 2006

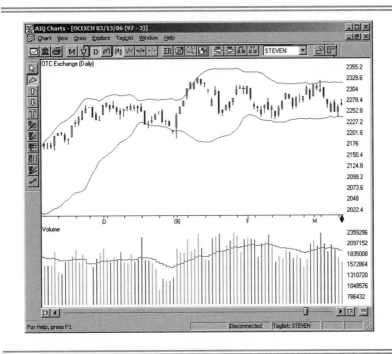

Courtesy of AIQ

UPTREND MARKET

The third market condition is an uptrend, such as the market experienced during the period of 08/11/06 to 11/17/06, as shown in Figure 3.8. Running the basic bearish engulfing pattern with a three day holding period during this bullish market period resulted in 2,627 trades that showed an annualized ROI of negative 69%. Less than 37% of the trades were profitable and the trading pattern lost money on more than 62% of the trades. This was the worst result so far.

The test results are interesting and show that in these cases the bearish engulfing pattern works best in a downtrending market and should be avoided in sideways or uptrending markets. Testing the basic bearish engulfing pattern in another market downtrend, the period between 07/28/05 and

BULLISH MARKET DURING AUGUST TO NOVEMBER 2006

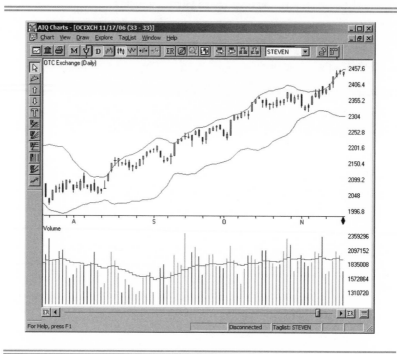

Courtesy of AIQ

10/17/05, confirms the previous results by showing a 38% annualized ROI for the 1,451 trades made. More than 54% of the trades were profitable.

After testing the bearish engulfing trading pattern in two different time frames and all three types of market conditions, we find that the only times it has shown profitable annualized ROIs were the two times it was tested in bearish markets. Additional testing bears out the results that this trading pattern works best in declining markets and provides poor results in trading range or bullish markets.

Many trading patterns show specific market environments in which they perform well; and others where they are best avoided. One of the keys to trading involves knowing which is which. Unless traders study the results of large numbers of trades in different market conditions, they will not know when to use each pattern in their trading toolbox. Using the same pattern in all market conditions may just churn the account. Selecting the right pattern for the current market conditions may improve trading results.

VARYING THE HOLDING PERIOD

Table 3.1 shows the effect of varying the holding period for the basic bearish engulfing pattern when running the test during the market downtrend of 12/31/04 to 04/28/05. The best results are obtained using a four day holding period and the annualized ROI drops off consistently for longer holding times. The bearish engulfing pattern is a short term trading pattern and the longer the position is held, the lower the results. Each trading pattern seems to have time frames that it likes best. It is a good idea to check this information for every pattern you intend to use.

TABLE 3.1
TEST RESULTS FOR 12/31/04 TO 04/28/05
WITH DIFFERENT HOLDING PERIODS

HOLDING PERIOD	ANNUALIZED ROI	WINNING PERCENTAGE
3 Days	31.63%	58.36%
4 Days	38.06%	59.13%
5 Days	30.35%	58.01%
6 Days	29.34%	57.73%
7 Days	22.58%	56.71%

CONTINUING THE INVESTIGATION—
EFFECT OF DIFFERENT FILTERS

Up to this point, our testing has established that traders should consider focusing bearish engulfing trades on periods when the market is in a downtrend. Knowing the market environment in which to use a trading pattern is critical. Now we will investigate the effects of different filters on the basic bearish engulfing pattern to see if there are ways to improve the trading results.

DOLLAR VALUE

For some trading patterns, the dollar value of the stock can influence the trading results. In order to investigate the effect of stock price on the bearish engulfing pattern, we ran the backtest during the 12/31/04 to 04/28/05 period using a price filter. The results are shown in Table 3.2. Each set of data is based on a three day holding period.

For this test period, the percent of winning trades and the annualized ROI generally increased as the closing value of the stock rose. The number of trades decreased with each increase in price. In Table 3.2 there are 1,256 trades when limiting the bearish engulfing pattern to stocks above $20. This decreases to 64 trades when considering only bearish engulfing trades in stocks priced above $70 during the test period.

We would obviously expect the number of trades to decrease as the trade candidates are limited to higher and higher prices. Sixty-four trades in four months are still enough to be statistically significant, and the interesting thing about Table 3.2 is that the winning percentage consistently increased as we limited trades to higher dollar-value stocks.

The price of the stock is something we may want to consider when taking trades. If further testing uncovers better filters, we may not use price as a factor because multiple filters can reduce the number of trades in the test period to something that is not statistically significant. We want to examine several different filters and then select the ones that provide the most leverage with the lowest reduction in the number of potential trades available. In the case where a particular day presented me with more trades than I wanted to take, I could always use the price level to prioritize the trading possibilities.

TABLE 3.2
TEST RESULTS FOR 12/31/04 TO 04/28/05
WITH DIFFERENT PRICE LEVELS

CLOSING PRICE	ANNUALIZED ROI	WINNING PERCENTAGE
20	34.15%	59.63%
30	38.94%	60.58%
40	32.86%	60.98%
50	51.43%	63.24%
60	62.74%	68.38%
70	102.83%	76.56%

VOLUME

Another filter that often affects trading patterns is volume. Volume measures the interest in a stock. Stocks that are moving up on increasing volume are showing that more people are willing to pay more money for the stock every day, just the kind of thing you want to own. Stocks that are moving up on less volume every day indicate that fewer people are willing to pay more money for the stock, and perhaps it is time to take profits.

The average volume shows the overall interest in a stock. High volume stocks have institutional support almost by definition. Lower volume stocks are often not followed by institutions because they must take large positions and cannot get in and out easily. In order to determine if the average daily trading volume affects the results of trading the bearish engulfing pattern, I ran the backtest for the 12/31/04 to 04/28/05 period seven times with a different minimum average trading volume requirement each time. The average volume is computed as the simple moving average of daily volume over a 21 day period. The results are shown in Table 3.3.

The results are different from those of the price testing shown in Table 3.2. When we increased the minimum price requirement for taking a bearish engulfing trade, the winning percentage increased every time. When the average volume requirement for taking a bearish engulfing pattern trade was increased, the results were not smooth. Sometimes they increased between volume levels and sometimes they decreased.

TABLE 3.3
TEST RESULTS FOR 12/31/04 TO 04/28/05
WITH DIFFERENT AVERAGE DAILY VOLUME REQUIREMENTS

AVERAGE TRADING VOLUME	ANNUALIZED ROI	WINNING PERCENTAGE
200,000	36.64%	58.13%
400,000	35.77%	57.47%
600,000	35.12%	57.34%
800,000	34.39%	55.77%
1,000,000	40.95%	54.92%
2,000,000	25.07%	54.28%
3,000,000	35.57%	56.22%

Table 3.3 indicates that there is not a strong enough correlation between the average daily trading volume and the test results to use average volume as a factor in selecting trades. Backtesting is valuable not only for how it finds ways to leverage a trading pattern, but also because it shows you factors that you do not need to consider. In the case of the bearish engulfing pattern, we have found that results are better when trading higher dollar stocks and that the average daily volume does not have a significant effect on results.

FIRST DAY VERSUS SECOND DAY VOLUME

The next filter tested for the bearish engulfing pattern is the volume on the day the bearish engulfing occurs. Does it matter if the second day of the pattern occurs on above average volume? An example of a high volume

FIGURE 3.9:
HIGH VOLUME BEARISH ENGULFING IN FDX ON 3/15/05

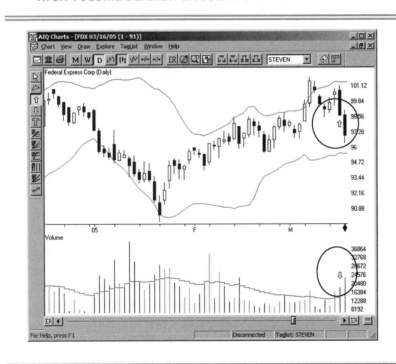

Courtesy of AIQ

bearish engulfing pattern is shown in Figure 3.9 where the second day of the pattern is marked with an up arrow and the high volume on the day is marked by a down arrow.

In order to answer this question, I ran the backtest during the 12/31/04 to 04/28/05 period and added a filter describing the relationship of the volume on the second day of the pattern to the 21 day simple moving average of the volume. The results are shown in Table 3.4. The standard three day holding time was used for all positions.

The bearish engulfing pattern is looking to short an uptrending stock after a down day occurs that has a body whose range completely covers or engulfs the previous day's range. One would think that taking trades when this down day occurs on large volume would be good since the large volume might also indicate that the down day (the second day of the pattern) was more important. The test results of Table 3.4 indicate that, at least for this test period, this is not the case.

TABLE 3.4
TEST RESULTS FOR 12/31/04 TO 04/28/05
WITH DIFFERENT DAY TWO VOLUME RATIOS

DAY 2 VOLUME RATIO	ANNUALIZED ROI	WINNING PERCENTAGE
0.6	21.29%	56.48%
0.8	17.88%	57.35%
1.0	19.79%	58.38%
1.2	12.25%	58.32%
1.4	19.59%	54.64%
1.6	48.80%	50.26%

There are many ideas that seem logical for trading patterns. Some of these work, many do not. This is why testing trading patterns before using them is important. It is much better to find out what really works instead of trading on beliefs and assumptions. The data in Table 3.4 indicates that, in general, above average volume on the second day of a bearish engulfing pattern hurts rather than helps results.

TABLE 3.5
TEST RESULTS FOR 12/31/04 TO 04/28/05
WITH DAY 2 VOLUME LARGER THAN DAY 1 VOLUME

DAY 2 VOLUME	ANNUALIZED ROI	WINNING PERCENTAGE
No Requirement, Standard Test	31.63%	58.36%
0.7 times Day One volume	42.81%	58.42%
0.9 times Day One volume	51.62%	58.91%
1.1 times Day One volume	51.81%	59.47%
1.2 times Day One volume	59.67%	61.17%
1.3 times Day One volume	65.86%	62.14%
1.4 times Day One volume	72.07%	63.34%

If instead of looking for a volume increase compared to the average daily volume, we simply look for larger volume on the second day of the bearish engulfing pattern than we had on the first day of the pattern, the results are much more promising. The data in Table 3.5 shows the results of running the backtest seven times during the period of 12/31/04 to 04/28/05 using a constant three day holding period for each test.

The first line in Table 3.5 shows the results of the standard bearish engulfing pattern during this test period. The second line adds a requirement to the standard pattern that the volume on the second day of the pattern be at least 70% of the volume that occurred on the first day of the pattern. The third line in Table 3.5 shows the test results for the standard pattern with the additional requirement that the second day's volume be at least 90% of the first day's volume.

It is interesting to note that when the second day's volume is at least 130% of the volume on the first day of the pattern, the annualized ROI in the tests doubles over that found when using the basic pattern. The relationship between the first day's volume (the volume on the white bar up day) and the volume on the second day of the pattern (the black bar down day) is clearly important to results.

FIGURE 3.10:
UNH BEARISH ENGULFING, FIRST DAY OF
PATTERN A RECENT HIGH

Courtesy of AIQ

Another suggestion by some traders is to only take bearish engulfing pattern trades when the first day of the pattern is a recent high in the stock. The idea here is that the bearish engulfing pattern would occur at recent highs. An example of this pattern is shown in Figure 3.10, which shows the bearish engulfing pattern that occurred in UNH on 04/08/05. UNH had been in a brief run up, and the first day of the bearish engulfing pattern occurred at the high for the run. The second day of the pattern marked the beginning of a retracement in UNH and trading this pattern would have been quite profitable.

FIRST DAY AS A RECENT HIGH

As noted before, traders need to be very careful when shown a few examples of a trading pattern that "works." A few examples provide just enough

FIGURE 3.11:
TEST RESULTS FOR FIRST DAY OF PATTERN BEING A RECENT HIGH

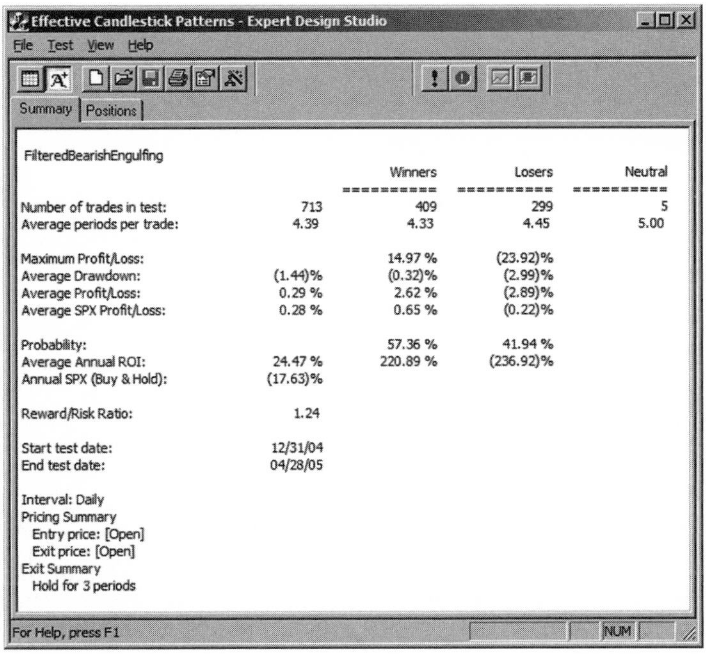

		Winners	Losers	Neutral
Number of trades in test:	713	409	299	5
Average periods per trade:	4.39	4.33	4.45	5.00
Maximum Profit/Loss:		14.97 %	(23.92)%	
Average Drawdown:	(1.44)%	(0.32)%	(2.99)%	
Average Profit/Loss:	0.29 %	2.62 %	(2.89)%	
Average SPX Profit/Loss:	0.28 %	0.65 %	(0.22)%	
Probability:		57.36 %	41.94 %	
Average Annual ROI:	24.47 %	220.89 %	(236.92)%	
Annual SPX (Buy & Hold):	(17.63)%			
Reward/Risk Ratio:	1.24			
Start test date:	12/31/04			
End test date:	04/28/05			

Courtesy of AIQ

information to get you into trouble. I am more interested in how the pattern has performed over several hundred or a thousand trades than in seeing just a few successful examples. Backtesting the bearish engulfing pattern with the requirement that the first day of the pattern be a recent high yields the results shown in Figure 3.11.

Figure 3.11 indicates that adding the requirement to the basic bearish engulfing pattern that the first day of the pattern also be a recent high as shown in Figure 3.10 reduces performance. The basic pattern performs better than the version with this additional requirement.

The entire bearish engulfing pattern testing to this point has focused on testing filters external to the pattern itself, such as price, volume, and the position of the pattern in the stock's trend. Based on this testing, we have found that the bearish engulfing pattern works best when the general market, as measured by the NASDAQ, is in a downtrend and does not work well when the general market is uptrending or in a trading range. We have also found that the pattern works better on higher-priced stocks and with a holding period of three to four days.

AMOUNT OF OVERLAP

Now we will look at how slight variations in the bearish engulfing pattern itself affect trading results during the market downtrend of 12/31/04 to 04/28/05. The basic bearish engulfing pattern just requires that the second day's black body overlap the first day's white body—any amount of overlap is OK. The next test looks to see how the results are affected by requiring a larger overlap.

Figure 3.12 shows a bearish engulfing pattern that occurred in SNDA on 12/31/2004 and is noted by the up arrow in the chart. The top of the second day's black body (marked by the up arrow) extends at least 15% of the day's range above the top of the previous day's body. In the basic bearish engulfing pattern definition, the second day's body just needs to be above the top of the first day's body. The new definition we are going to test requires that the top of the second day's body be at least 15% of the day's range higher than

Courtesy of AIQ

the top of the body in the first day of the pattern, as illustrated by the SNDA pattern in Figure 3.12.

Figure 3.13 shows the test results during the 12/31/04 to 04/28/05 NASDAQ downtrend using the modified bearish engulfing pattern. This new requirement of "top overlap" improves both the annualized ROI and the percentage of winning trades.

"Bottom overlap" is the requirement that the bottom of the second day's body extend at least 15% of the day's range below the bottom of the first day's body. Modifying the basic bearish engulfing pattern to require just bottom

```
┌─────────────────────────────────────────────────────────────────────────┐
│ ⚡ Effective Candlestick Patterns - Expert Design Studio          _ □ X   │
│ File  Test  View  Help                                                    │
│ ┌──┐┌──┐ ┌─┐┌─┐┌─┐┌─┐┌─┐┌─┐              ┌─┐┌─┐ ┌─┐┌─┐                     │
│ │□ ││A'││□││ ││ ││ ││ ││ │              │!││0│ │ ││ │                     │
│ └──┘└──┘ └─┘└─┘└─┘└─┘└─┘└─┘              └─┘└─┘ └─┘└─┘                     │
│ ┌Summary┐┌Positions┐                                                      │
│                                                                           │
│   FilteredBearishEngulfing                                                │
│                                        Winners        Losers      Neutral │
│                                      ==========    ==========  ========== │
│   Number of trades in test:       778      470           304          4   │
│   Average periods per trade:      4.29     4.27          4.32       4.00   │
│                                                                           │
│   Maximum Profit/Loss:                  19.20 %      (26.38)%             │
│   Average Drawdown:          (1.30)%    (0.30)%      (2.85)%             │
│   Average Profit/Loss:         0.47 %     2.61 %      (2.81)%             │
│   Average SPX Profit/Loss:     0.25 %     0.59 %      (0.27)%             │
│                                                                           │
│   Probability:                          60.41 %      39.07 %             │
│   Average Annual ROI:         40.35 %  222.48 %     (237.84)%             │
│   Annual SPX (Buy & Hold):   (17.63)%                                     │
│                                                                           │
│   Reward/Risk Ratio:           1.43                                       │
│                                                                           │
│   Start test date:          12/31/04                                      │
│   End test date:            04/28/05                                      │
│                                                                           │
│   Interval: Daily                                                         │
│   Pricing Summary                                                         │
│     Entry price: [Open]                                                   │
│     Exit price: [Open]                                                    │
│   Exit Summary                                                            │
│     Hold for 3 periods                                                    │
│                                                                           │
│ ┌───────────────────────────────────────┬──────────────┬─────────┐       │
│ │For Help, press F1                      │              │NUM      │       │
│ └───────────────────────────────────────┴──────────────┴─────────┘       │
└─────────────────────────────────────────────────────────────────────────┘
```

Courtesy of AIQ

overlap does not improve results and in fact reduces the annualized ROI when tested in the 12/31/04 to 04/28/05 NASDAQ downtrending market.

Based on this testing, it appears that a strong initial up move on the second day of the pattern that then reverses—resulting in a down day—is more beneficial to trading results than "bottom overlap." I also tested whether a long upper shadow on either day one or day two of the pattern affected the backtesting results. Neither one improved the annualized ROI during the test period.

COMBINING FILTERS

Table 3.6 summarizes the results of testing the bearish engulfing pattern. It is rarely advisable to just combine all the things that improve results, since this typically reduces the number of trades to a statistically insignificant number. However, one can sometimes combine a couple of filters and still have a significant number of trades and an improved trading pattern.

TABLE 3.6
SUMMARY OF TEST RESULTS FOR BEARISH
ENGULFING PATTERN DURING NASDAQ DOWNTREND

FILTER	ANNUALIZED ROI	WINNING PERCENTAGE
No Filter, Standard Test	31.63%	58.36%
Increasing Holding to 4 days	38.06%	59.13%
Requiring Close to Be > $50	51.43%	63.24%
Average Volume > 800K	34.39%	55.77%
Day 2 Volume > average	19.79%	58.38%
Day 2 Volume 1.3 times Day 1	65.86%	62.14%
First Day Is Recent High	24.47%	57.36%
Upper Body Overlap	40.35%	60.41%

TEST RESULTS COMBINING THE TWO TOP FILTERS OF TABLE 3.6

```
Effective Candlestick Patterns - Expert Design Studio          _□×
File  Test  View  Help

□ A  □ ☞ ⊟ ⎙ ☜ ▧              ! 0  ⊠ ▣
Summary | Positions

FilteredBearishEngulfing
                                     Winners        Losers        Neutral
                                   ==========    ==========    ==========
Number of trades in test:       78         53            24             1
Average periods per trade:    4.15       4.09          4.25          5.00

Maximum Profit/Loss:                     7.76 %      (10.84)%
Average Drawdown:            (0.86)%     (0.13)%      (2.50)%
Average Profit/Loss:          0.56 %      1.98 %      (2.56)%
Average SPX Profit/Loss:      0.50 %      0.95 %      (0.48)%

Probability:                            67.95 %       30.77 %
Average Annual ROI:          48.82 %    176.27 %     (219.93)%
Annual SPX (Buy & Hold):    (17.63)%

Reward/Risk Ratio:            1.71

Start test date:            12/31/04
End test date:              04/28/05

Interval: Daily
Pricing Summary
  Entry price: [Open]
  Exit price: [Open]
Exit Summary
  Hold for 3 periods

For Help, press F1                                      NUM
```

Courtesy of AIQ

Combining the best two filters from Table 3.6 would seem logical, but let's test it. The sixth filter shown in Table 3.6 required the volume on the second day of the bearish engulfing pattern to be at least 1.3 times the volume of the first day of the pattern. Using this filter with the basic bearish engulfing pattern resulted in an annualized ROI of 65%. The third filter shown in Table 3.6 required the stock to have a price more than $50. Using only this filter resulted in an annualized ROI of 51%. Combining these two filters resulted in an annualized ROI of 48%, as shown in Figure 3.14. Combining two strong filters actually reduced the annualized ROI.

Filters interact in ways that are not obvious, and traders need to test combinations of filters just as they test individual filters to determine which ones are the best to use. At this point we have determined that the bearish engulfing trading pattern works best when used in periods when the NASDAQ is in a downtrend and when selecting patterns that have volume on the second day greater than 1.3 times the volume on the first day. The next step in testing the pattern is to verify that this filter is also beneficial during other downtrending periods in the NASDAQ.

Table 3.7 shows the test results for the basic bearish engulfing pattern and the pattern with the additional requirement that the volume on the second day of the pattern be at least 1.3 times the volume of the first day. Note that during each of the periods shown in Table 3.7, the market was in a downtrend and a buy and hold strategy would have lost significant money.

The results shown in Table 3.7 are interesting in that during four different market downtrends, the basic bearish engulfing trading pattern was a profitable trading system when the market moved down. It also shows that in each of those periods, adding the volume filter improved the trading results.

TABLE 3.7
BEARISH ENGULFING PATTERN TEST
RESULTS IN DIFFERENT MARKET DOWNTRENDS

MARKET DOWNTREND PERIOD	ROI STANDARD PATTERN	ROI WITH FILTER
05/05/06 to 07/20/06	126.49	170.87
03/08/05 to 04/20/05	62.25	79.40
07/02/04 to 08/13/04	73.98	81.30
01/26/04 to 03/24/04	51.74	81.38

FINAL RESULTS—HOW TO
TRADE THE BEARISH ENGULFING

After examining thousands of bearish engulfing patterns in different market conditions and using various filters, the test results presented here indicate that the results of the bearish engulfing pattern may be improved by: using it in downtrending or bearish markets, using a three to five day holding period, using it on higher-priced stocks, looking for volume on the second day of the pattern that is larger that the volume on the first day of the pattern, and taking patterns when the top of the second day's body is at least 15% of the day's range above the top of the first day's body.

The test results also indicate that results may be diminished using the bearish engulfing pattern in the following conditions: when the NASDAQ is uptrending or bullish, holding positions more than six days, patterns with above average volume on the second day, when the first day of the pattern is a recent high, patterns where the bottom of the second day's body is more than 15% below the bottom of the first day's body.

The improved Bearish Engulfing pattern requirements are:

- The stock must be in an uptrend.
- The NASDAQ must be in a downtrend.
- The first day of the pattern shows a white body.
- The second day of the pattern shows a black body that overlaps the first day's body.
- The second day volume is at least 30% above the first day's volume.

CHAPTER 4

HAMMER PATTERNS

The hammer pattern may mark a reversal of a stock's downtrend. Hammers have long lower shadows or tails, short or no upper shadows, and small bodies. They actually look like a hammer, with the long tail being the handle and the small body being the head of the hammer. The color of the body is not considered important; it can be either a white or black body, implying the hammer can occur on either an up or down day.

The most common definition requires the lower shadow to be twice the length of the body, or more. The common definitions indicate there should be no or very little upper shadow showing and the day's high should be near the close for a white body and near the open for a black body. One of the advantages of backtesting a potential trading pattern is that we can investigate this definition and determine things like whether the color of the body matters, whether different lengths of the lower shadow affect results, and just how small the upper shadow has to be.

Figure 4.1 shows a hammer pattern in EXBD that occurred on 07/14/06 and is marked by the down arrow on the chart. EXBD had been in a clear downtrend, as marked by a series of lower highs and lower lows, for 10 weeks. On 07/14/06, the stock moved down after the open, which is the bottom of the body on a white candlestick, and then retraced the move to close up for the day. This trading action left a long lower shadow, which is more than twice the length of the body, and a small upper shadow that completed the definition of a hammer pattern. After forming the hammer pattern, EXBD moved up more than $3 in the next few trading sessions.

Hammers can also have a black body, indicating they closed down for the day. The only requirements are a small upper shadow and a lower shadow that is more than twice the length of the body. Figure 4.2 shows a black-bodied hammer that occurred in PHI on 06/28/06 and is marked by the up arrow on the chart.

FIGURE 4.1:
HAMMER PATTERN IN EXBD ON 7/14/06

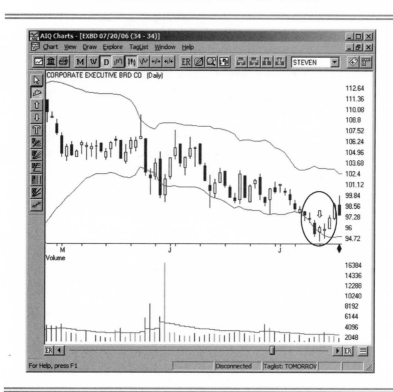

Courtesy of AIQ

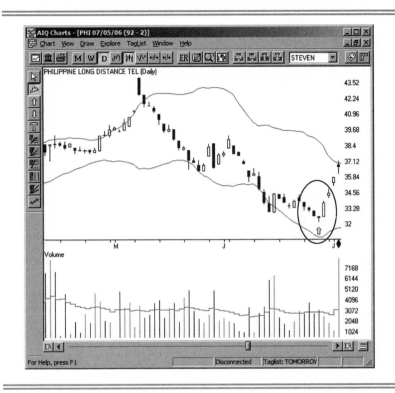

Courtesy of AIQ

PHI had been in a downtrend for two months when, on 06/28/06, it opened down and continued moving down. Later in the day, it rallied and closed near the highs of the day, forming a long lower shadow and a black body. During the next four trading sessions, PHI ran up over 13%.

DETERMINING THE OPTIMAL
PATTERN DEFINITION—SHADOWS

The requirement in the hammer definition that the pattern have a small or no upper shadow is not well defined. In order to backtest the pattern, we need a specific definition. I chose to start with the requirement that the upper shadow be less than 15% of the day's trading range. The good thing about backtesting is that we can easily test a range of lengths for the upper shadow to determine if it makes a significant difference, and if it does, we can then determine which is the best one to use.

INITIAL TEST PERIOD: 1/3/06 TO 5/1/07

Figure 4.3 shows a hammer with a large upper shadow (marked by the down arrow) that occurred in ZF on 04/18/05. In order to determine if larger upper shadows affect the trading results of the hammer pattern, we can use backtesting techniques.

The backtest results of Figure 4.4 were obtained by looking at all the hammers that occurred in downtrending stocks during the period of 01/03/06 to 05/01/07. When a hammer pattern formed, a trade was entered the next day at the opening price, held for five days, and sold. The tests were run on

FIGURE 4.3:
HAMMER WITH LARGE UPPER SHADOW IN ZF ON 4/18/05

Courtesy of AIQ

a database of about 2,200 stocks that comprise trading candidates that have an average daily volume greater than 200,000 shares plus most of the sector ETFs. This is the database from which I trade. A stock with lower average daily volumes may have wide bid/ask spreads and can be hard to enter and exit quickly.

Figure 4.4 indicates that hammer patterns occur quite frequently since the backtest took more than 3,800 positions during the 1½-year test period. The basic pattern shows an annualized ROI of slightly over 10%. This sounds interesting until you notice that the annualized ROI for trading the SPX during the same period was slightly over 14%. Our first pass indicated that during this test period the hammer pattern, as defined, is not something I would trade. However, backtesting techniques allow us to explore how this pattern works in different market conditions and also if changes in the basic definition would improve results.

FIGURE 4.4:
INITIAL BACKTEST OF HAMMER PATTERN

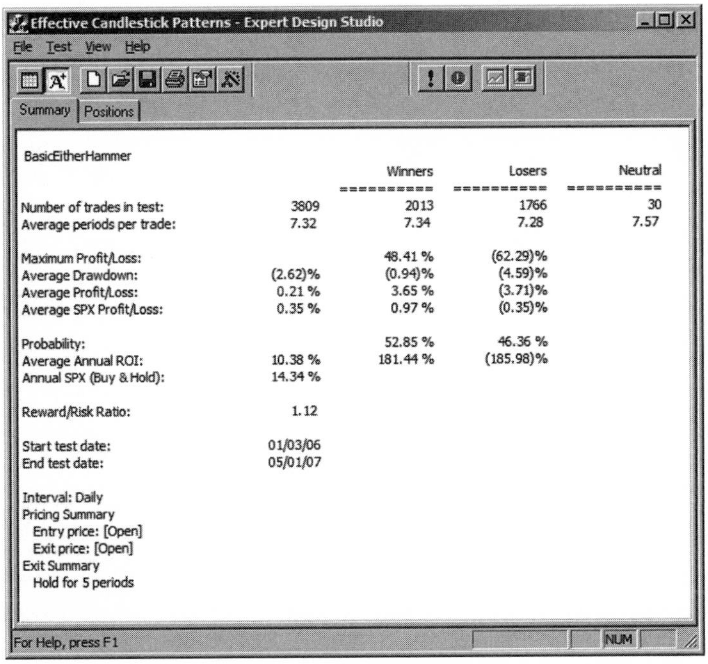

Effective Candlestick Patterns - Expert Design Studio

File   Test   View   Help

Summary | Positions

BasicEitherHammer

		Winners	Losers	Neutral
Number of trades in test:	3809	2013	1766	30
Average periods per trade:	7.32	7.34	7.28	7.57
Maximum Profit/Loss:		48.41 %	(62.29)%	
Average Drawdown:	(2.62)%	(0.94)%	(4.59)%	
Average Profit/Loss:	0.21 %	3.65 %	(3.71)%	
Average SPX Profit/Loss:	0.35 %	0.97 %	(0.35)%	
Probability:		52.85 %	46.36 %	
Average Annual ROI:	10.38 %	181.44 %	(185.98)%	
Annual SPX (Buy & Hold):	14.34 %			
Reward/Risk Ratio:	1.12			
Start test date:	01/03/06			
End test date:	05/01/07			

Interval: Daily
Pricing Summary
  Entry price: [Open]
  Exit price: [Open]
Exit Summary
  Hold for 5 periods

For Help, press F1   NUM

Courtesy of AIQ

The hammer definition does not clearly define what "little or no" upper shadow means, so that is a reasonable place to begin our investigation of the pattern. The test results of Figure 4.4 used a requirement that the upper shadow be less than 15% of the day's trading range. Examining the results of testing different upper shadow length requirements will help us understand what works best.

One of the important aspects of trading patterns is to make sure they are clearly defined. When a pattern definition contains adjectives such as big or small, it leaves room for interpretation in the definition. When there is room for interpretation, traders using the same pattern may see different results due to the interpretation issues.

DIFFERENT UPPER SHADOW LENGTHS

Table 4.1 shows the effect of different upper shadow lengths on the test results of the hammer pattern during the 01/03/06 to 05/01/07 testing period. For this particular test period, it appears that reducing the upper shadow length reduces annualized ROI. Rather than requiring the hammer pattern to have little or no upper shadow, the results of Table 4.1 indicate we should consider hammers whose upper shadow length is 20% or less of the day's trading range.

Since the initial results indicate that shorter upper shadows actually reduce returns of the hammer pattern and since this result was unexpected, I decided to run the tests in a different time period. I also ran a test that was twice as long. If results are similar in different time periods, they are more likely to be correct.

Table 4.2 shows the results of testing the hammer pattern during the three-year period of 01/01/04 to 12/29/06. This data leads to several interesting conclusions. First, since the number of trades increased in rough proportion to the increase in the testing time frame, it would appear that hammer patterns are a regular occurrence through different time frames and market conditions. This is a positive result, since patterns that occur infrequently or are found only in one time frame may be event-driven rather than a natural part of market activity.

TABLE 4.1
EFFECT OF UPPER SHADOW LENGTH ON
HAMMER RESULTS DURING 1/03/06 TO 5/01/07

UPPER SHADOW LENGTH	ANNUALIZED ROI	NUMBER OF TRADES
25% of Day's Range	15.35%	5,901
20% of Day's Range	15.58%	4,930
15% of Day's Range	10.38%	3,809
10% of Day's Range	8.43%	2,709
5% of Day's Range	6.26%	1,686
1% of Day's Range	<0.23%>	1,077

TABLE 4.2
EFFECT OF UPPER SHADOW LENGTH ON
HAMMER RESULTS DURING 1/01/04 TO 12/29/06

UPPER SHADOW LENGTH	ANNUALIZED ROI	NUMBER OF TRADES
25% of Day's Range	16.39%	13,466
20% of Day's Range	16.22%	11,318
15% of Day's Range	12.59%	8,942
10% of Day's Range	9.55%	6,656
5% of Day's Range	8.29%	4,366
1% of Day's Range	1.06%	2,987

The second interesting result of comparing the data in Table 4.1 and 4.2 is that the annualized ROIs were similar. This indicates that in different time periods and market conditions, the pattern performs about the same. This gives confidence that the returns are not driven by specific things that just occurred in one time frame and hence may not repeat in the future.

The third interesting result of comparing the data in Table 4.1 and 4.2 is that in both test periods the annualized ROI decreased consistently as the upper shadow length was decreased. This lends credibility to the thought that when using hammer patterns, we should allow upper shadow lengths of up to 20% of the day's trading range.

Since the data in Tables 4.1 and 4.2 indicate that the annualized ROI decreases as the upper shadow length requirement decreases, it raises an interesting

FIGURE 4.5:
HAMMER BACKTEST WITH UPPER SHADOW >5% AND <20% OF DAY'S RANGE

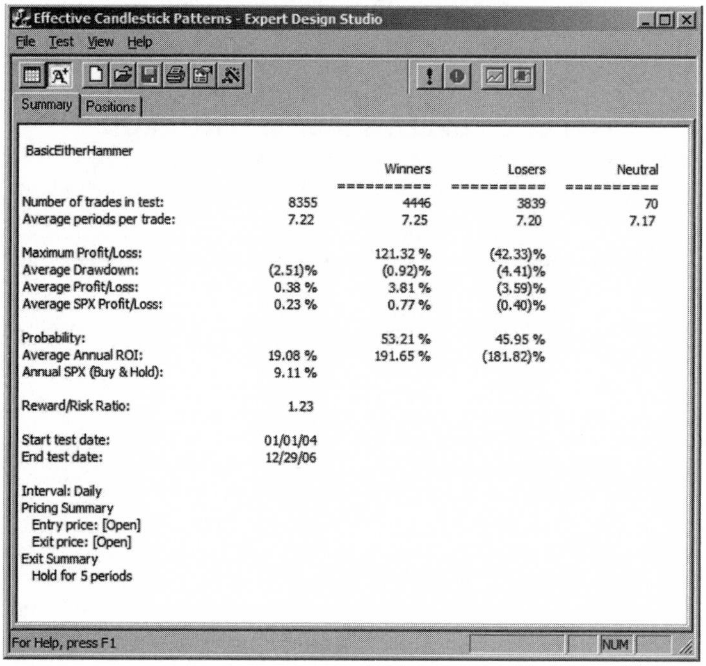
Effective Candlestick Patterns - Expert Design Studio

File Test View Help

Summary | Positions

BasicEitherHammer

		Winners	Losers	Neutral
Number of trades in test:	8355	4446	3839	70
Average periods per trade:	7.22	7.25	7.20	7.17
Maximum Profit/Loss:		121.32 %	(42.33)%	
Average Drawdown:	(2.51)%	(0.92)%	(4.41)%	
Average Profit/Loss:	0.38 %	3.81 %	(3.59)%	
Average SPX Profit/Loss:	0.23 %	0.77 %	(0.40)%	
Probability:		53.21 %	45.95 %	
Average Annual ROI:	19.08 %	191.65 %	(181.82)%	
Annual SPX (Buy & Hold):	9.11 %			
Reward/Risk Ratio:	1.23			
Start test date:	01/01/04			
End test date:	12/29/06			

Interval: Daily
Pricing Summary
Entry price: [Open]
Exit price: [Open]
Exit Summary
Hold for 5 periods

For Help, press F1 NUM

Courtesy of AIQ

question. What happens if we require hammer patterns to have an upper shadow length of at least 5% of the day's range, and less than 20% of the day's range? This test result is shown in Figure 4.5.

UPPER SHADOWS BETWEEN 4 AND 20%

Figure 4.5 indicates that testing the hammer during the three-year period of 2004, 2005, and 2006 shows improved results by adding a requirement that the upper shadow in the pattern be between 4% and 20% of the day's trading range. This new requirement filters out hammer patterns with small upper shadows between 0 and 4% of the day's trading range. It improves the annualized ROI as compared to just a requirement that the upper shadow be less than 20% of the day's trading range. It appears that the hammer pattern works best with at least a small upper shadow.

TESTING BODY COLOR

Part of the hammer definition is that the body color does not matter. Hammers can have either white or black bodies. As the famous quote goes, "Trust but verify." This is also good advice for traders. I want to test every part of a pattern's definition to be sure I really understand it and also that each part of the definition is relevant to results. Again, backtesting does not guarantee future results, but I am more interested in trading patterns that have worked well in the past than ones that have no information other than a few successful examples.

I tested whether the body color of the pattern matters by separately backtesting hammers with black bodies and hammers with white bodies. The test period used was the same as for the tests above, the years 2004, 2005, and 2006. The tests included the requirement that the upper shadow of the hammer be less than 20% of the day's trading range. No restriction was placed on the minimum upper shadow length.

During the period of 01/01/04 to 12/29/06, hammers with upper shadows less than 20% of the day's trading range and black bodies showed an annualized ROI of 17.82% when using a five-day holding period. During the same test period and using the same five-day holding time, hammers with white bodies showed a 12.4% annualized ROI. This difference indicates that during this time period, the body color of the hammer pattern affects the trading results.

In order to double-check this result, I retested the black body and white body hammer patterns in a different time period. During the test period of 01/03/06 to 05/01/07, black-bodied hammers with an upper shadow less than 20% of the day's trading range resulted in a 7.79% annualized ROI. During the same test period, white-bodied hammers yielded a 21.63% annualized ROI.

Testing the effects of hammer body color in the second time period showed opposite results. During the 01/03/06 to 05/01/07 test period, white bodied hammers outperformed black bodied hammers. This is an illustration of why test results should always be checked in multiple time frames before drawing any conclusions. The interesting result is that body color does seem to affect the trading results, but it can affect it either way. Unless we found another factor that resulted in more consistent performance, it appears best to stick with the standard definition and trade hammers of both body colors.

Backtesting gathers evidence and traders must view the evidence as a jury would. Usually not every piece of evidence is lined up for just the prosecution or defense. There is often some positive evidence for each side. However, when the preponderance of evidence supports one conclusion, then that is usually the one to believe. When test results in different time periods yield significantly different results, then the particular filter being tested is not likely to be a key factor in results. When testing in different time periods leads to the same conclusions, then they are more likely to be correct.

USING A PRICE FILTER

Table 4.3 shows the results of testing a price filter during the 01/01/04 to 12/29/06 time period. The results indicate that price may be a factor in the returns for the hammer pattern and when given a choice, traders may want to pick patterns occurring in stocks under $30.

TABLE 4.3
EFFECT OF CLOSING PRICE ON
HAMMER RESULTS DURING 1/01/04 TO 12/29/06

CLOSE GREATER THAN	ANNUALIZED ROI	NUMBER OF TRADES
10	15.62	9,197
20	16.20	6,274
30	13.11	3,777
40	9.25	2,197
50	2.52	1,177

TESTING THE EFFECT OF A VOLUME FILTER

Volume characteristics often affect the results of trading patterns. I usually focus on trading stocks with at least an average daily volume of 100,000 shares. I use the 21 day simple moving average for determining average volume. The reason for not trading most stocks whose average daily volume is less than 100,000 shares is that they often have wide bid/ask spreads and may be hard to get out of if the market suddenly turns.

Table 4.4 shows the results for testing the hammer pattern during the 01/01/04 to 12/29/06 time period using different volume filters. In each case, the 21 day simple moving average of the volume is required to be above 100,000 and below the number in the first column. The test data indicates that the hammer pattern works best on stocks with average daily volumes under a million shares. All tests were run allowing either black or white candlestick bodies and upper shadows less than 20% of the day's trading range.

When I share trading pattern data in my newsletter, *The Timely Trades Letter*, or in live seminars, someone usually asks why patterns favor certain price or volume characteristics. Backtesting does not tell you why trading patterns favor certain filters; it just indicates that within the test period they do. Answers like large volume stocks are harder to move, or small volume stocks can move quicker satisfy people, but may or may not be the reason.

Trading is a statistical business. It is really not possible to know if any particular trade will be profitable, and to keep looking for the magic indicator that will always lead you to profitable trades is a losing game. I study each potential trading pattern in order to understand whether it has performed well in the past, and, if so, what market conditions and filters are most helpful.

Volume relationships affect the profitability of many trading patterns, but not always in the same way. Just because a particular volume pattern has helped one trading pattern does not imply it will help others. Each pattern must be tested on its own. Table 4.5 shows the results of requiring that the volume on the day of the hammer pattern be a different multiple of the previous day's volume.

The basic hammer pattern (either white or black bodies and requiring an upper shadow of at least 4% of the day's trading range but not more than 20%) showed an annualized ROI during the 01/01/04 to 12/29/06 time period of 16%, as shown in Table 4.5. The annualized ROI for buying and holding the SPX was slightly over 9%, indicating that there was some advantage to trading the hammer pattern. If we only took hammer trades when the volume on the day of the hammer was at least as much as the previous day's volume, the percentage of winning trades remained the same, but the annualized ROI moved up to almost 22%, as shown on the third line of Table 4.5.

TABLE 4.4
EFFECT OF MINIMUM AVERAGE
VOLUME ON HAMMER RESULTS DURING 1/01/04 TO 12/29/06

AVERAGE VOLUME LESS THAN	ANNUALIZED ROI	NUMBER OF TRADES
3,000,000	17.04	8,949
2,000,000	18.09	8,220
1,000,000	21.49	6,504
800,000	23.57	5,792
600,000	25.76	4,740
400,000	27.43	3,355

TABLE 4.5
EFFECT OF INCREASED VOLUME OVER
PREVIOUS DAY ON RESULTS DURING 1/01/04 TO 12/29/06

VOLUME PERCENT OF PREVIOUS DAY	ANNUALIZED ROI	WINNING PERCENTAGE
No Volume Requirement	16.22%	53%
80%	16.70%	53%
100%	21.91%	54%
120%	22.66%	54%
140%	21.90%	53%
160%	21.88%	53%

Annualized ROI versus Percentage of Winners

Many traders focus only on the annualized ROI number, and feel that bigger is better. However, the percentage of winning trades is also important in actual trading. If a trading system wins about 50% of the time, then over the course of 256 trades there is a reasonable chance of seeing eight losing trades in a row. The number of losing trades in a row relates to drawdown and how much of the account should be risked on any given trade. A trading pattern with a higher percentage of winning trades would be likely to show fewer consecutive losing trades.

If a trader does not realize that it would be normal for this pattern to see eight losing trades in a row at some point during 256 consecutive trades, he or she may see several losing trades and feel that the pattern is no longer effective, then move on to another pattern. But if the trader understands that with a trading system that wins near 50% of the time, he or she should expect to see eight losing trades in a row, he or she can adjust position sizes to control drawdown to a tolerable level. The better understanding the trader has about how his various trading patterns perform, the more effective use the trader can make of them.

Table 4.6 shows the data for testing the relationship between the volume on the day of the hammer and the 21 day simple moving average of the stock's volume. This relationship is stronger than the relationship to the previous day's volume. The last line in Table 4.6 indicates that the annualized ROI doubles during this test period when trades are restricted to hammers that occur with volume greater than 160% of the 21 day simple moving average.

It is not often that you find a filter that doubles the annualized ROI for a trading pattern, so when this happens I must check the results in another time frame and make sure there are enough trades during the period to be statistically significant.

TABLE 4.6
EFFECT OF INCREASED VOLUME OVER
AVERAGE ON RESULTS DURING 1/01/04 TO 12/29/06

VOLUME PERCENT OF AVERAGE VOLUME	ANNUALIZED ROI	WINNING PERCENTAGE
No Volume Requirement	16.22%	53%
80%	19.65%	53%
100%	23.57%	54%
120%	25.94%	53%
140%	30.58%	53%
160%	35.99%	53%

During the three-year test period, the results showed that when taking only hammers occuring with at least 160% of the average volume, there were 1,545 trades. This is enough to be significant, and is likely more than any trader would actually take.

Running the same test during the 01/03/06 to 05/01/07 time period showed a 27% annualized ROI, which was nearly double the 14% annualized of

BasicEitherHammer		Winners	Losers	Neutral
Number of trades in test:	648	367	275	6
Average periods per trade:	7.30	7.27	7.35	7.00
Maximum Profit/Loss:		26.70 %	(58.18)%	
Average Drawdown:	(2.93)%	(1.08)%	(5.46)%	
Average Profit/Loss:	0.55 %	4.04 %	(4.10)%	
Average SPX Profit/Loss:	0.52 %	1.01 %	(0.12)%	
Probability:		56.64 %	42.44 %	
Average Annual ROI:	27.32 %	202.69 %	(203.43)%	
Annual SPX (Buy & Hold):	14.34 %			
Reward/Risk Ratio:	1.31			
Start test date:	01/03/06			
End test date:	05/01/07			

Interval: Daily
Pricing Summary
  Entry price: [Open]
  Exit price: [Open]
Exit Summary
  Hold for 5 periods

Courtesy of AIQ

buy and hold for the SPX. The test results (shown in Figure 4.6) compared favorably to the 15% return during the same period when no volume requirement was used. Based on these tests covering a 5½-year period, it appears the hammer pattern benefits by adding this volume requirement to the basic definition.

REVISED DEFINITION MEANS NEW TESTS

This volume filter works well enough that I have incorporated it into my standard hammer pattern definition. I will use this as the starting definition in subsequent testing. Adding a filter to the hammer will subsequently imply that it is being added to and compared with the new standard definition unless stated otherwise:

- The stock must be in a downtrend.
- The upper shadow must be more than 4% and less than 20% of the day's range.
- The body can be either black or white.
- The volume must be more than 160% of the 21 day average.

While I was writing this chapter, a friend suggested that hammers worked better if the range on the day the hammer occurs is wider than the recent day's ranges. One of the great things about backtesting is that when someone gives you a trading idea, instead of just risking your money on someone else's feeling, you can test it to see if the suggestion has merit.

RANGE TEST

I added a filter to the new hammer definition defined above that required the range (the high value minus the low value for the day) on the day of the hammer to be the largest range in the past five days. The test results for this filter during the 01/03/06 to 05/01/07 time period are shown in Figure 4.7. During this test period, taking only wide range hammers increased the annualized ROI from 27% to 48%. It also increased the percentage of winning trades from 56% to more than 58%. Wide range hammers are an interesting idea, not because my friend suggested it, but because it tests well. The wide range hammer also showed 222 trades during this 16-month test.

In order to verify this result was not limited to specific events during the test period, I also ran the test during the three-year period of 01/01/04 to 12/29/06. This resulted in a 44.71% annualized ROI, slightly less than 54% winning trades, and 391 trades during the period. Running the test in the same period without the wide range filter yielded a 29% annualized ROI and 52% winning trades with 1,128 trades taken.

Since the wide range hammer filter nearly doubles annualized ROI in tests involving two different time frames and covering almost five years, it appears to be something worth considering in trading the hammer pattern. An example hammer with the wide range filter is shown in Figure 4.8, in which the hammer is marked by the down arrow. Notice that the hammer's

TEST RESULTS FOR HAMMER RANGE
THE LARGEST OF THE LAST FIVE SESSIONS

```
Effective Candlestick Patterns - Expert Design Studio          _ □ X
File  Test  View  Help

[toolbar icons]                              [toolbar icons]
Summary | Positions |

BasicEitherHammer
                                    Winners      Losers      Neutral
                                   =========   =========   =========
Number of trades in test:      222       130          88            4
Average periods per trade:     7.27      7.22         7.35        7.00

Maximum Profit/Loss:                   26.70 %      (23.57)%
Average Drawdown:            (2.72)%    (1.02)%      (5.37)%
Average Profit/Loss:          0.96 %     4.36 %      (4.01)%
Average SPX Profit/Loss:      0.51 %     0.89 %      (0.03)%

Probability:                           58.56 %      39.64 %
Average Annual ROI:          48.42 %   220.51 %    (198.98)%
Annual SPX (Buy & Hold):     14.34 %

Reward/Risk Ratio:            1.61

Start test date:            01/02/06
End test date:              05/01/07

Interval: Daily
Pricing Summary
  Entry price: [Open]
  Exit price: [Open]
Exit Summary
  Hold for 5 periods

For Help, press F1                              NUM
```

Courtesy of AIQ

range is the largest range in the last five trading sessions and that there was a significant volume spike on the day the hammer occurred.

When I develop trading patterns for my trading toolbox, I always want to know how they perform in different market conditions. I determine this by testing the patterns in bullish markets, bearish markets, and trading range markets. In actual practice, I use trend lines on the NASDAQ to determine the condition the market is in and when it is changing.

RANGE TEST IN A SIDEWAYS TRENDING MARKET

During the first three months of 2006, the market was stuck in a trading range, as shown in Figure 4.9. Trading range markets can be difficult for

WIDE RANGE HAMMER IN CHTR ON 03/14/06

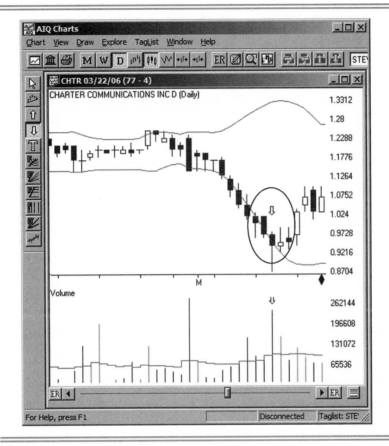

Courtesy of AIQ

traders, since stocks tend to trigger out of setups less often and when they do, they tend to "pop and drop." This happens almost by definition because, if most stocks were triggering and running, then the market, which is the sum of the stocks, would have to be trending and not range-bound.

Taking all wide range hammer trades during this period resulted in 19 trades; a 135% annualized ROI, and 68% winning trades, as shown in Figure 4.10. During a short period, annualized ROI can be a misleading, but bigger is better. The interesting part of Figure 4.10 is the 68% winning trades number. When I find a system that wins more than 60% of the time, I am interested. The question is whether this holds up in other trading range markets.

NASDAQ TRADING RANGE IN EARLY 2006

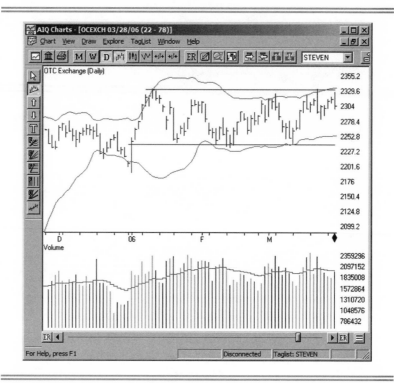

Courtesy of AIQ

The market was also in a trading range during the period of 11/14/06 to 02/14/07. Testing the wide range hammer pattern during this period resulted in 25 trades with a 43% annualized ROI as compared to 20% for buy and hold. Of the 25 trades during this period, 68% were winners.

The trading range market of 01/07/05 to 03/14/05 showed 43 wide range hammer trades resulting in a 73% annualized ROI as compared to 8% for buy and hold. Testing the pattern during this period showed 62% winning trades.

Testing the wide range hammer during the 10/03/03 to 12/29/03 trading range market resulted in only six trades; and showed a negative annualized ROI of 18%, with only 33% winning trades. The pattern generated very few

WIDE RANGE HAMMER TEST RESULTS IN 2006 TRADING RANGE

Effective Candlestick Patterns - Expert Design Studio			
File Test View Help			
Summary Positions			
BasicEitherHammer	Winners	Losers	Neutral
Number of trades in test:	19	13	6	0
Average periods per trade:	7.21	7.08	7.50	0.00
Maximum Profit/Loss:		20.31 %	(7.14)%	
Average Drawdown:	(1.64)%	(0.36)%	(4.42)%	
Average Profit/Loss:	2.68 %	5.64 %	(3.75)%	
Average SPX Profit/Loss:	0.39 %	0.46 %	0.25 %	
Probability:		68.42 %	31.58 %	
Average Annual ROI:	135.43 %	291.01 %	(182.63)%	
Annual SPX (Buy & Hold):	8.27 %			
Reward/Risk Ratio:	3.26			
Start test date:	01/04/06			
End test date:	03/28/06			

Interval: Daily
Pricing Summary
  Entry price: [Open]
  Exit price: [Open]
Exit Summary
  Hold for 5 periods

For Help, press F1   NUM

Courtesy of AIQ

trades during this period, and they did not work well. Very few patterns work all the time.

The wide range hammer pattern worked well in three of the four trading range markets shown here. In the cases in which it worked, it performed well and generated a number of trades. In the one case in which it did not perform well, it only generated a few trades. This reinforces the thought that there are no guarantees in trading and traders need to adjust position sizing and risk levels to reflect the fact that losses do occur.

RANGE TEST IN BULL MARKETS

In bull markets such as the 03/14/07 to 05/09/07 period, the wide range hammer pattern seems to perform well, as shown in Figure 4.11. The annualized ROI is better than buy and hold and the winning percentage is 76%. The pattern also performed well during the 07/24/06 to 11/24/06 uptrending market, where it showed an annualized ROI of twice buy and hold and 43 trades, of which 60% were winners.

The wide range hammer pattern did not perform well during the market's bull move from 10/13/05 to 12/05/05. During this period, the backtesting showed 45 trades yielding only 7% annualized ROI, while buy and hold showed 47%. Once again, there are times when trading patterns do not work. Successful traders find patterns that work most of the time and focus their trading during favorable market conditions for each specific pattern. They

FIGURE 4.11:
WIDE RANGE HAMMER TEST RESULTS FOR 3/14/07 TO 5/09/07

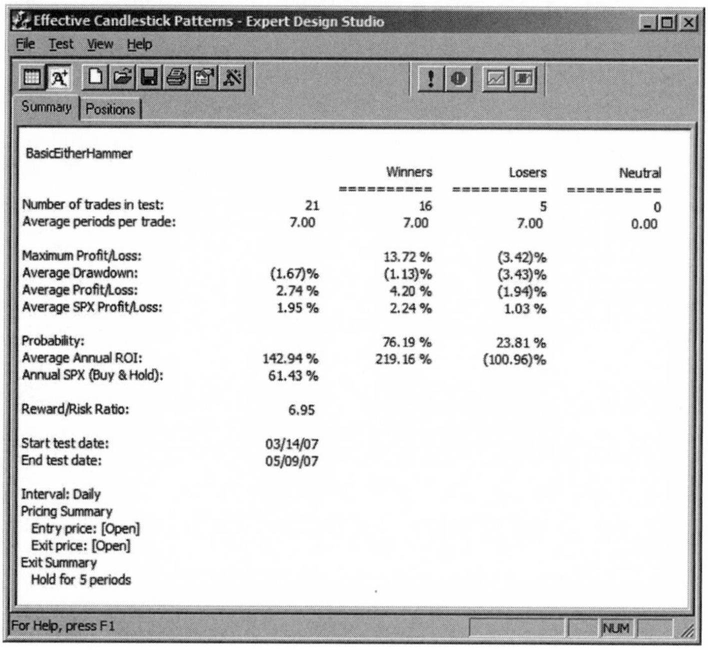

Courtesy of AIQ

also make sure that position sizing and money management techniques are used that allow them to get by the inevitable periods when trading is going through a losing streak.

RANGE TEST IN BEAR MARKETS

I found the wide range hammer generally does not test well during periods when the market is in a downtrend. During the 03/08/05 to 04/29/05 market downtrend, the pattern lost an annualized ROI of 42%, which was more than buy and hold lost during the same period, as shown in the test results of Figure 4.12. The pattern generated 41 trades and only had a winning percentage of 34%. Other testing indicates that while the pattern performs OK in some downtrends, it is typically a good idea not to trade it when the market is bearish.

FIGURE 4.12:
WIDE RANGE HAMMER TEST IN MARKET DOWNTREND

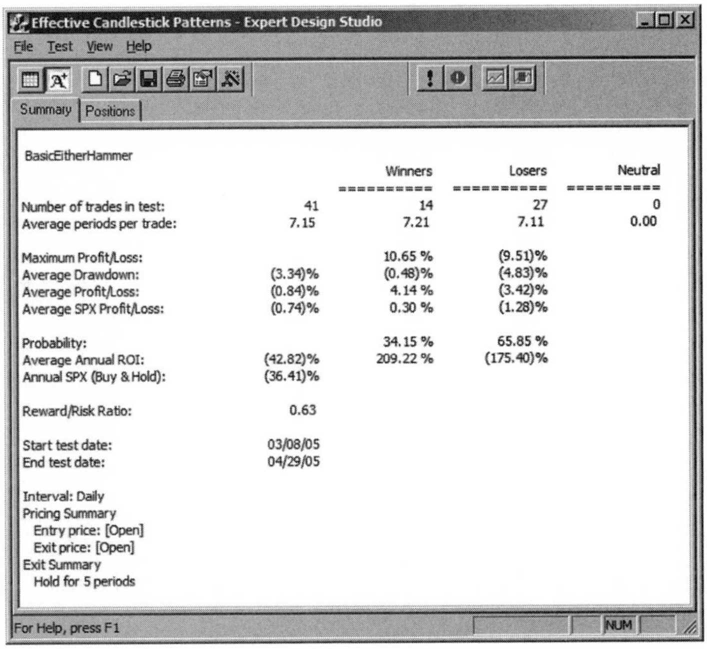

Effective Candlestick Patterns - Expert Design Studio

File Test View Help

Summary | Positions

BasicEitherHammer

		Winners	Losers	Neutral
Number of trades in test:	41	14	27	0
Average periods per trade:	7.15	7.21	7.11	0.00
Maximum Profit/Loss:		10.65 %	(9.51)%	
Average Drawdown:	(3.34)%	(0.48)%	(4.83)%	
Average Profit/Loss:	(0.84)%	4.14 %	(3.42)%	
Average SPX Profit/Loss:	(0.74)%	0.30 %	(1.28)%	
Probability:		34.15 %	65.85 %	
Average Annual ROI:	(42.82)%	209.22 %	(175.40)%	
Annual SPX (Buy & Hold):	(36.41)%			
Reward/Risk Ratio:	0.63			
Start test date:	03/08/05			
End test date:	04/29/05			

Interval: Daily
Pricing Summary
Entry price: [Open]
Exit price: [Open]
Exit Summary
Hold for 5 periods

For Help, press F1 NUM

Courtesy of AIQ

FINAL RESULTS—HOW TO TRADE THE HAMMER PATTERN

After examining thousands of hammer patterns in different market conditions and using various filters, the test results presented here indicate that the results of the hammer pattern may be improved by: requiring the upper shadow be at least 5% of the day's range, trading stocks priced under $30, trading stocks with average daily volume under one million shares, trading when volume is 160% or more of the previous day's volume, trading hammers whose range is the largest range of the last 5 days.

The test results also indicate that results may be diminished using the hammer pattern in the following conditions: when the NASDAQ is downtrending or bearish, when hammers have an upper shadow less than 4% of the day's range, trading stocks with prices above $50, trading when volume is less than the previous day's volume.

The improved hammer pattern requirements are:

- The stock must be in a downtrend.
- The NASDAQ must be in an uptrend or wide trading range.
- The upper shadow must be greater than 4% and less than 20% of the day's range.
- The lower shadow must be greater than twice the body length.
- The body may be either white or black.
- The volume must be more then 160% of the 21 day average.
- The range of the hammer must be the largest range in the last five days.

CHAPTER 5

HANGING MAN PATTERNS

The hanging man pattern may mark a reversal of a stock's uptrend. Hanging man patterns look just like hammers except that they occur after a stock has been in an uptrend. Hanging man patterns have long lower shadows or tails, short or no upper shadows, and small bodies. The color of the body is not important. The lower tail should be twice the length of the body or more. There should be no or very little upper shadow, indicating the day's high should be near the close for a white body and near the open for a black body.

Since the hanging man may occur at the end of an uptrend, traders attempt to profit from the pattern by entering short positions and then covering the position after a few days. In a short sale, the trader borrows stock from the broker and sells it, then buys it back on the open market to close out the position and return the borrowed stock.

Figure 5.1 shows a hanging man pattern that occurred in CME on 11/27/06. CME had broken out of a base and started moving up. On Nov. 27, CME

FIGURE 5.1:
HANGING MAN PATTERN IN CME ON 11/27/06

Courtesy of AIQ

FIGURE 5.2:
HANGING MAN PATTERN IN DPHIQ ON 10/27/06

Courtesy of AIQ

formed a hanging man as marked by the down arrow. The hanging man pattern marked the end of the uptrend, as during the next five trading sessions CME dropped about 18 points.

Another example of a hanging man pattern is shown in Figure 5.2. DPHIQ had been in an uptrend until the hanging man formed on 10/27/06 when the day's trading formed a black body with a small upper shadow and a long lower shadow. This hanging man pattern marked the end of the uptrend and an opportunity for a 20% gain from a short position.

Of course no trading pattern works all the time and when the hanging man does not mark the end of an uptrend and the stock keeps rising, traders will lose money in a short position. Figure 5.3 shows a hanging man that occurred on 04/26/06 in HSOA. The pattern is the same; the stock had been in an uptrend and then, on April 26, the trading activity formed a long lower

FIGURE 5.3:
FAILED HANGING MAN PATTERN IN HSOA ON 04/26/06

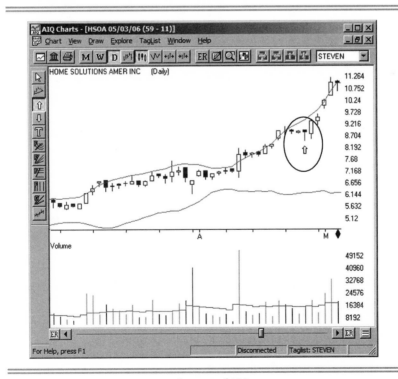

Courtesy of AIQ

shadow with a small upper shadow, yet the stock kept going up over the next five sessions.

BACKTESTING THE BASIC PATTERN

From these examples we know that sometimes the hanging man trading pattern works and sometimes it does not. Traders need to see hundreds or thousands of trades in order to determine how often a particular pattern works, in which market conditions it works best, and when to avoid using it. The AIQ Systems' backtesting program examined all the hanging man patterns that occurred between 01/03/06 and 05/01/07 and produced the results shown in Figure 5.4.

FIGURE 5.4:
HANGING MAN INITIAL BACKTEST
DURING 1/03/06 TO 5/01/07

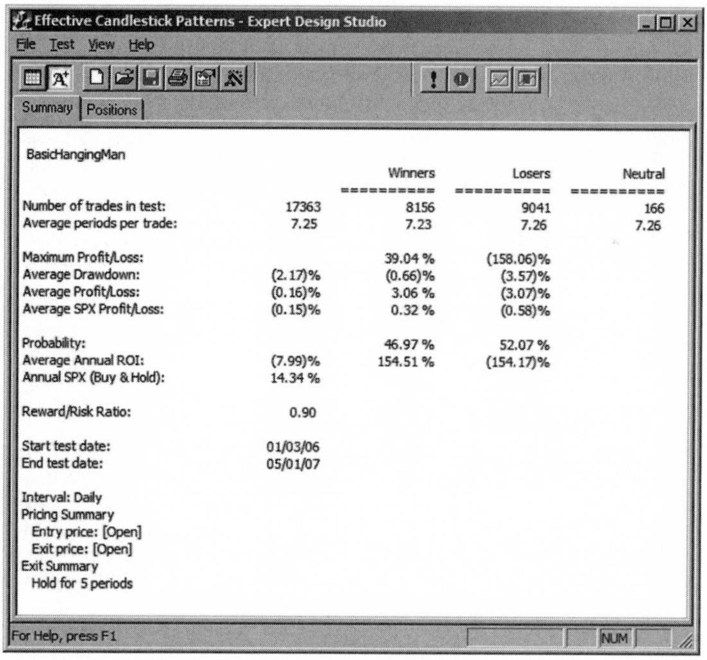

Effective Candlestick Patterns - Expert Design Studio

File   Test   View   Help

Summary | Positions |

BasicHangingMan

		Winners	Losers	Neutral
Number of trades in test:	17363	8156	9041	166
Average periods per trade:	7.25	7.23	7.26	7.26
Maximum Profit/Loss:		39.04 %	(158.06)%	
Average Drawdown:	(2.17)%	(0.66)%	(3.57)%	
Average Profit/Loss:	(0.16)%	3.06 %	(3.07)%	
Average SPX Profit/Loss:	(0.15)%	0.32 %	(0.58)%	
Probability:		46.97 %	52.07 %	
Average Annual ROI:	(7.99)%	154.51 %	(154.17)%	
Annual SPX (Buy & Hold):	14.34 %			
Reward/Risk Ratio:	0.90			
Start test date:	01/03/06			
End test date:	05/01/07			

Interval: Daily
Pricing Summary
  Entry price: [Open]
  Exit price: [Open]
Exit Summary
  Hold for 5 periods

For Help, press F1   NUM

Courtesy of AIQ

During the period between 01/03/06 and 05/01/07, there were more than 17,000 hanging man patterns. The basic pattern is very common. The results were not favorable; the pattern showed winning trades only about 47% of the time and, if all trades were taken, resulted in an annualized net loss of about 8%. Buying and holding the SPX during the test period showed a net gain of more than 14%. Clearly in this specific time period, traders would not want to rely on the basic hanging man pattern.

While the initial test results are not encouraging, one test period does not prove anything. Examining all of the hanging man patterns in a period more than twice as long, 01/01/04 to 05/01/07, also yielded disappointing results, as shown in Figure 5.5. The results were similar to the initial test period. Taking all the hanging man trades during this period resulted in an annualized net loss of 13% and again about 47% of the trades were profitable.

FIGURE 5.5:
HANGING MAN BACKTEST DURING 01/013/04 TO 5/01/07

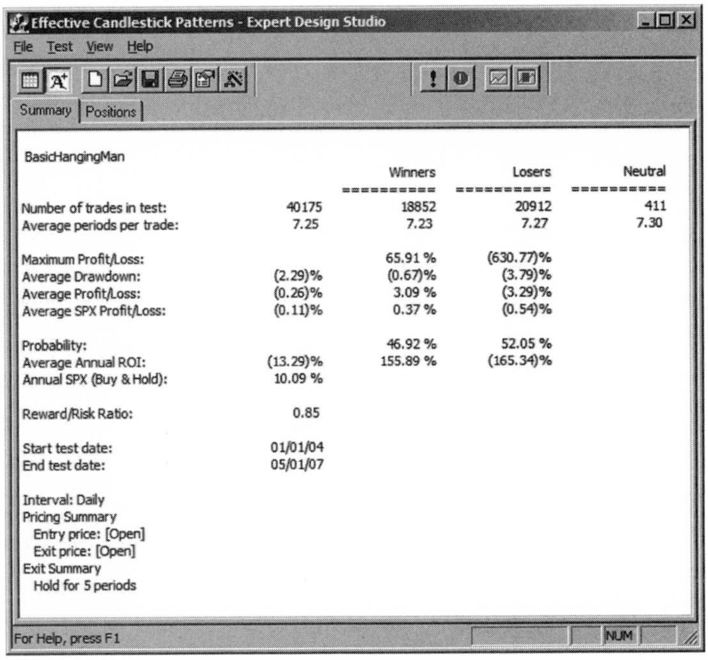

Effective Candlestick Patterns - Expert Design Studio				_ □ ×
File Test View Help				

Summary | Positions

BasicHangingMan		Winners	Losers	Neutral
Number of trades in test:	40175	18852	20912	411
Average periods per trade:	7.25	7.23	7.27	7.30
Maximum Profit/Loss:		65.91 %	(630.77)%	
Average Drawdown:	(2.29)%	(0.67)%	(3.79)%	
Average Profit/Loss:	(0.26)%	3.09 %	(3.29)%	
Average SPX Profit/Loss:	(0.11)%	0.37 %	(0.54)%	
Probability:		46.92 %	52.05 %	
Average Annual ROI:	(13.29)%	155.89 %	(165.34)%	
Annual SPX (Buy & Hold):	10.09 %			
Reward/Risk Ratio:	0.85			
Start test date:	01/01/04			
End test date:	05/01/07			

Interval: Daily
Pricing Summary
  Entry price: [Open]
  Exit price: [Open]
Exit Summary
  Hold for 5 periods

For Help, press F1   NUM

Courtesy of AIQ

ADDING A VOLUME FILTER

Let's look at requiring a volume filter in the basic hanging man pattern. The first volume filter to be tested required that the volume on the day the hanging man occured be larger than the previous day's volume; yet, after testing, this requirement resulted in fewer trades than would be expected, but yielded about the same results. Therefore, when defined as above, this filter does not appear to be something useful.

Traders make their living by examining various trading patterns looking for a combination of patterns and filters that provide a statistical edge. Finding filters that do not work is helpful because the trader knows those characteristics may be ignored when looking at trading candidates.

Using a filter that requires the volume on the day the hanging man occurs to be above the 21 day simple moving average of the volume shows some improvement. The loss is cut in half and the winning percentage improves slightly. A loss is still a loss, so even though this filter results in a smaller loss, it would be better for the trader to not use the basic hanging man with this filter. Using multiples of 110% and 120% of the average volume did not significantly improve results either.

Filters Are Not One Size Fits All

It appears that large volume on the day the hanging man occurs is not an effective filter. Some patterns, such as certain types of pullback patterns, show improved results when using increased volume filters. This test data indicates that just because a filter helps one type of trading pattern, it does not mean it will help others. Traders need to be careful about applying filters that are recommended by others. I always want to test any idea to see how it has performed in the past before using it.

TESTING THE PATTERN
UNDER DIFFERENT MARKET CONDITIONS

Most trading patterns have market conditions in which they work well and other market conditions in which they do not work well at all. The initial test period of 01/03/06 to 05/01/07 shows bullish and bearish environments as shown in Figure 5.6.

FIGURE 5.6:
MARKET ENVIRONMENT DURING 1/03/06 TO 5/01/07

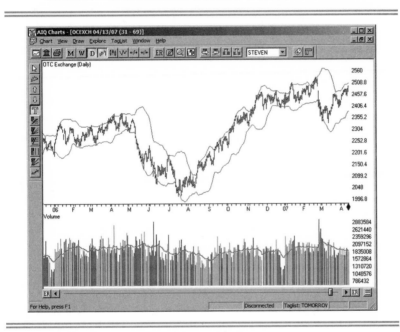

Courtesy of AIQ

BEAR MARKET TEST

The period between 05/05/06 and 07/21/06 was bearish and saw the NASDAQ dropping from the 2,350 area to the 2,015 area. During this period, the backtesting results showed 270 hanging man patterns with more than 79% of them resulting in profitable trades, as shown in Figure 5.7.

This is a very interesting result. In this particular bearish market, the hanging man was much more effective than in any of the previous tests that

FIGURE 5.7:
HANGING MAN TEST RESULTS DURING 5/05/06 TO 7/21/06

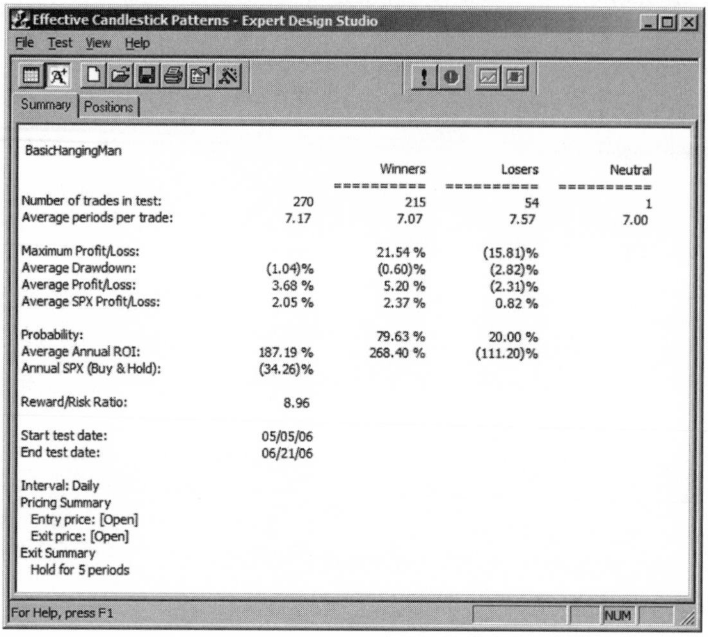

```
Effective Candlestick Patterns - Expert Design Studio                    _ □ X
File   Test   View   Help

□ A   □ ☞ 🖫 🖨 🖻 🖎                    ! ◐ ☑ ▣
Summary │ Positions │

  BasicHangingMan
                                          Winners      Losers        Neutral
                                       ===========  ===========   ===========
  Number of trades in test:      270         215           54              1
  Average periods per trade:    7.17        7.07         7.57           7.00

  Maximum Profit/Loss:                     21.54 %     (15.81)%
  Average Drawdown:            (1.04)%     (0.60)%      (2.82)%
  Average Profit/Loss:          3.68 %      5.20 %      (2.31)%
  Average SPX Profit/Loss:      2.05 %      2.37 %       0.82 %

  Probability:                            79.63 %      20.00 %
  Average Annual ROI:         187.19 %    268.40 %    (111.20)%
  Annual SPX (Buy & Hold):    (34.26)%

  Reward/Risk Ratio:            8.96

  Start test date:           05/05/06
  End test date:             06/21/06

  Interval: Daily
  Pricing Summary
     Entry price: [Open]
     Exit price: [Open]
  Exit Summary
     Hold for 5 periods

For Help, press F1                                          NUM
```

Courtesy of AIQ

encompassed both bullish and bearish periods. The annualized ROI for the buy and hold strategy showed a loss, while the hanging man showed a significant gain. As noted above, the test results for any single period may or may not be indicative of actual results, so further testing of the effectiveness of the hanging man pattern in bearish markets is required.

Testing the hanging man pattern during the market's bearish period of 07/28/05 to 10/17/05 showed good results with more than 59% winning trades and an annualized ROI of nearly 33% as compared to negative 16% for a buy and hold strategy during the same period. The NASDAQ was also in a clear downtrend during the five month period of 12/30/04 to 04/28/05, as shown in Figure 5.8. Test results indicate that during this time there were 1,032 hanging man patterns and taking all the trades would have resulted in nearly 57% winning trades. The annualized ROI for this period was 30%, as opposed to a negative 17% for buy and hold as shown in Figure 5.9.

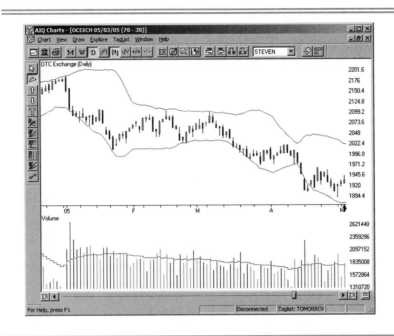

Courtesy of AIQ

FIGURE 5.9:

HANGING MAN RESULTS DURING BEAR
MARKET OF JAN. '04 TO MAY '05

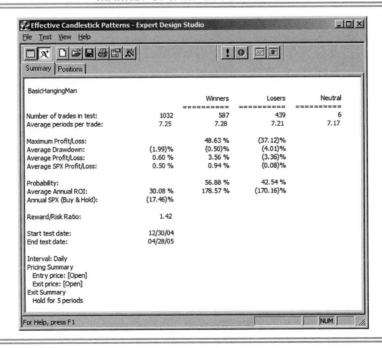

Courtesy of AIQ

Testing the hanging man pattern has shown that it performs poorly in periods when the market is moving through both bullish and bearish phases, and that it performs well in three different bearish environments. This does not prove that it will work well in all bearish market environments, but it does indicate that it is worth looking at in bearish markets.

FAILURE IN THE BULL MARKET

The initial test period of 01/03/06 to 05/01/07 for which the test results were negative, as shown in Figure 5.4, contained a bullish market period between 08/11/06 and 11/17/06. This bullish market period is shown in Figure 5.10, and the test results for this bullish period are shown in Figure 5.11. During this bullish period in the NASDAQ, the hanging man pattern only showed 41% winning trades and an annualized ROI of negative 28%, while buy and hold showed a positive 36% annualized ROI.

The market was also in a bullish period between 10/13/05 and 12/02/05. During this period, the test results indicated the hanging man pattern was only profitable on 34% of the trades and lost an annualized ROI of 55% as compared to a 52% annualized ROI gain for buy and hold. The hanging man continued to show good results in bearish markets, poor results in bullish markets, and mixed results in mixed markets. Based on these results, I would not trade the basic hanging man pattern in bullish environments and would consider it one of the tools in my toolbox during bearish markets.

REFINING THE TESTING

When testing different patterns and various filters, I am looking for clear and convincing evidence that the pattern has worked well and that filters have an obvious positive impact on results. Backtesting shows the results for trading all of the patterns that occur during the test period and the ROI is annualized. That's why traders will not see these exact numbers; they likely will not take every trade that presents itself and will usually not annualize their own results during short periods of time.

BULLISH MARKET PERIOD OF AUG. 2006 TO NOV. 2006

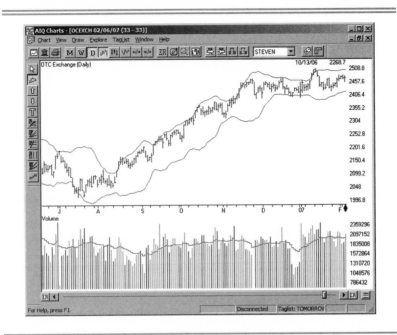

Courtesy of AIQ

HANGING MAN TEST RESULTS DURING
BULL RUN OF AUG. 2006 TO NOV. 2006

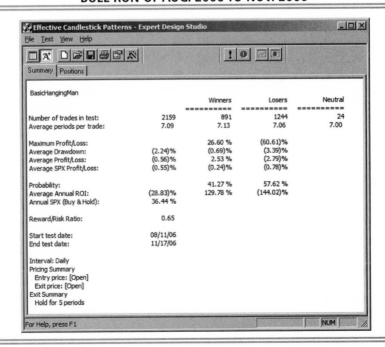

Courtesy of AIQ

If a filter, such as the volume ones tested previously, has test results that show a few points difference in annualized ROI or a few points difference in the percentage of winning trades, it does not mean much. When a pattern or filter shows dramatic improvements in several different test periods, then I have more confidence the results are due to characteristics of the pattern or filter. An example of this is the dramatic difference found between test results of the hanging man pattern in bullish and bearish market environments. This large and consistent difference is unlikely due to chance and more likely due to the effects of the market environment.

Now that we know the best market environment in which to use the hanging man pattern, we should look at several other filters to see if there are parameters of the pattern itself that strongly influence results. If there are, then we can use them to improve trading results. If we do not find any, then we can just focus on trading the basic pattern in bear markets.

PRICE FILTER

The basic hanging man pattern during the 01/03/06 to 05/01/07 test period yielded 47% winning trades and an 8% annualized ROI loss. Adding a requirement to the basic pattern to filter out all stocks with a closing price below $20 bumped up the annualized ROI to a loss slightly under 6% and left the winning percentage about the same. Neither of these results is the type of clear improvement we are looking for. The results were similar when adjusting the filter to eliminate all stocks with closing prices less than $40. The price level of the hanging man pattern does not appear to be a filter worth pursuing.

VOLUME FILTER

Table 5.1 shows the results of testing the hanging man pattern with a series of minimum average volume requirements. The tests were run during the same period of 01/03/06 to 05/01/07. The first column in Table 5.1 shows the minimum requirement for the 21 day simple moving average of the volume; the second column is the annualized ROI; the third column is the percentage of winning trades. The results do not provide a clear indication that traders should factor minimum average volume requirements into the trading decision.

TABLE 5.1
HANGING MAN TEST RESULTS
FOR MIN. AVG. VOL. DURING 01/03/06 TO 05/01/07

MIN. AVERAGE VOLUME	ANNUALIZED ROI	WINNING PERCENT
No Requirement	-7.99%	46.94%
500,000	-4.90%	47.49%
2,000,000	-2.97%	48.54%
5,000,000	-5.77%	48.80%
8,000,000	-8.96%	47.00%

HIGHEST HIGH REQUIREMENT

When looking at the actual positions traded during several of these tests, I noticed that in a number of cases the hanging man seemed to work when it occurred as a recent high. An example of this is shown in Figure 5.12, in which a hanging man occurred in ATI on 12/11/06, as marked by the down arrow. In this case, the day's high of the hanging man pattern was the highest high over five days.

Sometimes we notice things and it is just a fluke that several patterns worked with a particular characteristic. The only way to know if it is a coincidence or a real result is to test the characteristic in question. Figure 5.13 shows the results of testing the basic hanging man pattern during the 01/03/06 to 05/01/07 test period with the added requirement that trades are only taken if the high on the day the hanging man occurred was the highest high of the last five trading sessions.

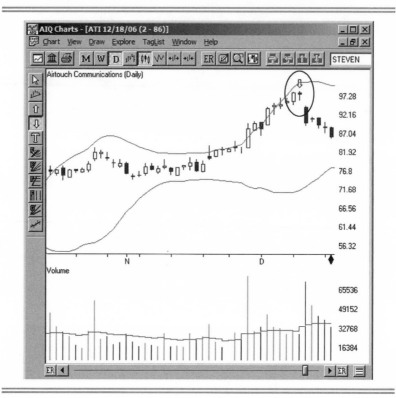

Courtesy of AIQ

The highest high of the last five day's requirement turned the hanging man pattern from a net loser during the test period into a net gainer. It also increased the winning percentage from 47% to more than 50%. The annualized ROI for the period was still below buy and hold; however, when a filter turns something from a net loss to a net gain and increases the winning percentage, it is worth noting.

During the testing process for the hammer pattern in Chapter four, we found that a filter for the widest range of the last five trading sessions improved the results. Using the same filter for the hanging man pattern during the test period of 01/03/06 to 05/01/07 produced the results shown in Figure 5.14. Once again, a filter that helps one trading pattern does not necessarily help a different pattern. Each trading pattern stands by itself, and filters must be tested with each different pattern.

**RESULTS FOR HANGING MAN IS
HIGHEST HIGH DURING JAN. 2006 TO MAY 2007**

Effective Candlestick Patterns - Expert Design Studio

File   Test   View   Help

Summary | Positions |

BasicHangingMan

		Winners	Losers	Neutral
Number of trades in test:	3906	1970	1895	41
Average periods per trade:	7.31	7.32	7.29	7.17
Maximum Profit/Loss:		33.28 %	(64.60)%	
Average Drawdown:	(1.78)%	(0.53)%	(3.11)%	
Average Profit/Loss:	0.15 %	2.87 %	(2.68)%	
Average SPX Profit/Loss:	0.05 %	0.41 %	(0.32)%	
Probability:		50.44 %	48.52 %	
Average Annual ROI:	7.31 %	143.05 %	(134.18)%	
Annual SPX (Buy & Hold):	14.34 %			
Reward/Risk Ratio:	1.11			
Start test date:	01/03/06			
End test date:	05/01/07			

Interval: Daily
Pricing Summary
    Entry price: [Open]
    Exit price: [Open]
Exit Summary
    Hold for 5 periods

For Help, press F1   NUM

Courtesy of AIQ

MACD OSCILLATOR AS A FILTER

It would be great if there were a couple of filters or, better yet, indicators that always improved trading results. There are hundreds of different indicators such as MACD, stochastic, relative strength, etc., that are available in charting packages. Many traders use these to time the market without having extensively tested them to see if they work. Some provide interesting results, many do not, but then that is a topic for another book.

As an example, some traders use the MACD or the MACD oscillator to time the market by trading long when the MACD oscillator is positive and trading short when the MACD oscillator is negative. In effect, they are looking for a bullish market when the MACD oscillator is positive and a bearish market when the MACD oscillator is negative.

Effective Candlestick Patterns - Expert Design Studio			

File   Test   View   Help

Summary | Positions

BasicHangingMan

		Winners	Losers	Neutral
Number of trades in test:	2488	1189	1280	19
Average periods per trade:	7.21	7.21	7.21	7.42
Maximum Profit/Loss:		33.37 %	(158.06)%	
Average Drawdown:	(2.22)%	(0.62)%	(3.74)%	
Average Profit/Loss:	(0.24)%	3.12 %	(3.36)%	
Average SPX Profit/Loss:	(0.22)%	0.22 %	(0.63)%	
Probability:		47.79 %	51.45 %	
Average Annual ROI:	(12.13)%	158.03 %	(170.22)%	
Annual SPX (Buy & Hold):	14.34 %			
Reward/Risk Ratio:	0.86			
Start test date:	01/03/06			
End test date:	05/01/07			

Interval: Daily
Pricing Summary
  Entry price: [Open]
  Exit price: [Open]
Exit Summary
  Hold for 5 periods

For Help, press F1

Courtesy of AIQ

We have found the basic hanging man pattern performs dramatically better in bearish markets than in bullish markets. So given that, some traders might think to use the MACD oscillator to time the market and determine when to take hanging man trades and when to avoid them.

Figure 5.15 shows the test results for the same 01/03/06 to 05/01/07 test period used in the initial backtest shown in Figure 5.4. Only taking trades when the MACD oscillator is less than zero during this period decreased both the annualized ROI and the percentage of winning trades. For this particular pattern and time frame, the MACD oscillator is not an effective timing tool. Once again, it is dangerous to assume something will work without first testing it.

One idea frequently used in trading patterns is that of confirmation. One form of confirmation is to look for a trading pattern, and then to not take the trade unless the stock is moving in the desired direction the next day.

Courtesy of AIQ

Since the hanging man is supposed to mark the end of an uptrend, we could look for the stock to be down the day following the occurrence of the pattern as confirmation. An example of this is shown in Figure 5.16, where the hanging man pattern occurred in WCC on 05/08/06 as noted by the up arrow. The next day, WCC closed down, which provided the confirmation, and the stock dropped 14% during the next three trading sessions.

The idea of confirmation can be tested by looking for hanging man patterns on day one, then requiring that on day two the close be lower than the close on day one. During the 01/03/06 to 05/01/07 test period, trading only confirmed hanging man patterns resulted in worse results than just trading the basic hanging man pattern. The test results are shown in Figure 5.17, and they indicate that the annualized ROI loss increased to more than 16% and the percentage of winning trades decreased to just more than 45%.

FIGURE 5.16:
HANGING MAN IN WCC WITH CONFIRMATION

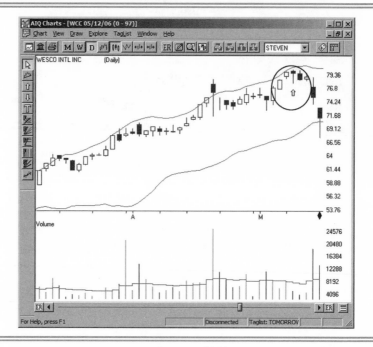

Courtesy of AIQ

FIGURE 5.17:
HANGING MAN WITH CONFIRMATION TEST RESULTS

Effective Candlestick Patterns - Expert Design Studio

File   Test   View   Help

Summary | Positions

ConfirmedHangingMan

		Winners	Losers	Neutral
Number of trades in test:	9967	4499	5385	83
Average periods per trade:	7.25	7.26	7.23	7.24
Maximum Profit/Loss:		50.18 %	(82.79)%	
Average Drawdown:	(2.27)%	(0.67)%	(3.63)%	
Average Profit/Loss:	(0.33)%	3.10 %	(3.20)%	
Average SPX Profit/Loss:	(0.15)%	0.42 %	(0.62)%	
Probability:		45.14 %	54.03 %	
Average Annual ROI:	(16.52)%	155.69 %	(161.29)%	
Annual SPX (Buy & Hold):	14.34 %			
Reward/Risk Ratio:	0.81			
Start test date:	01/03/06			
End test date:	05/01/07			

Interval: Daily
Pricing Summary
  Entry price: [Open]
  Exit price: [Open]
Exit Summary
  Hold for 5 periods

For Help, press F1

Courtesy of AIQ

DIFFERENT HOLDING PERIODS

Up to this point, all tests have used a five-day holding period. The position is entered at the opening the day after the hanging man pattern forms, held for five days, and then sold. Table 5.2 shows the results of using different holding periods. As holding periods decreased, the annualized ROI bounced around slightly but did not show a clear trend. The percentage of winning trades increased slightly every time the holding period was decreased.

TABLE 5.2
HANGING MAN HOLDING PERIOD
TEST RESULTS DURING 01/03/06 TO 05/01/07

HOLDING PERIOD	ANNUALIZED ROI	WINNING PERCENT
7 Days	-10.57%	45.36%
6 Days	-9.61%	46.89%
5 Days	-7.99%	46.97%
4 Days	-9.42%	47.55%
3 Days	-5.67%	48.33%
2 Days	-6.40%	48.73%

While the data shows a slight improvement in the percentage of winning trades for shorter holding times, experience tells me it is not significant enough to focus on. There are a number of different things that can influence actual trading results as compared to backtesting, such as the number of trades taken, slippage, the trader's risk tolerance, etc.

Because of these factors, I do not incorporate a parameter into my actual trading unless backtesting in multiple time frames shows clear and compelling evidence that the parameter strongly influences results. For example, trading the pattern only in bearish market environments or when the pattern occurs at the highest high of the last five days has been shown to strongly impact results and is worth factoring into my trading. A couple of points difference in the winning percentage are not enough to be useful on a practical basis.

MOVING AVERAGE TEST FEATURING THE 200 DAY

When shorting stocks, some traders like to look at tickers that are trading below their 200 day moving average. They feel that since some mutual funds ignore these stocks, there is less demand and they tend to drop easier. Like a lot of things we are told, it sounds interesting; however, in trading it is about what works.

Figure 5.18 shows the test results for all hanging man patterns that occurred below their 200 day simple moving average during the 01/03/06 to 05/01/07

FIGURE 5.18:
TEST RESULTS FOR HANGING MAN PATTERNS BELOW THEIR 200MA

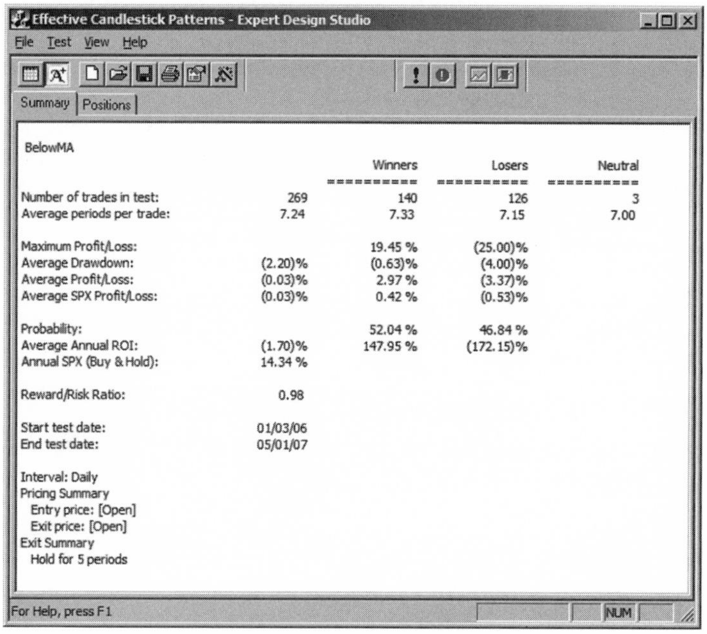

BelowMA

		Winners	Losers	Neutral
		==========	==========	==========
Number of trades in test:	269	140	126	3
Average periods per trade:	7.24	7.33	7.15	7.00
Maximum Profit/Loss:		19.45 %	(25.00)%	
Average Drawdown:	(2.20)%	(0.63)%	(4.00)%	
Average Profit/Loss:	(0.03)%	2.97 %	(3.37)%	
Average SPX Profit/Loss:	(0.03)%	0.42 %	(0.53)%	
Probability:		52.04 %	46.84 %	
Average Annual ROI:	(1.70)%	147.95 %	(172.15)%	
Annual SPX (Buy & Hold):	14.34 %			
Reward/Risk Ratio:	0.98			
Start test date:	01/03/06			
End test date:	05/01/07			

Interval: Daily
Pricing Summary
Entry price: [Open]
Exit price: [Open]
Exit Summary
Hold for 5 periods

Courtesy of AIQ

test period. Using the 200 day moving average as a filter significantly reduces the percentage of winning trades, and still results in a loss for the test period.

If instead of looking for hanging man patterns that occur below the 200 day simple moving average we look for patterns that form above short term moving averages, the test results are different. Table 5.3 shows the results of testing hanging man patterns between 01/03/06 and 05/01/07 and only taking trades when the stock closed above one of the short term moving averages listed.

TABLE 5.3
HANGING MAN MOVING AVERAGE
FILTER TEST RESULTS FOR 01/03/06 TO 05/01/07

CLOSE ABOVE MA	ANNUALIZED ROI	WINNING PERCENT
No Moving Average	-7.99%	46.97%
30	-7.87%	47.12%
20	-7.33%	47.30%
10	-2.67%	48.58%
5	-0.73%	48.93%

Taking trades that are above the 20 or 30 day moving averages does not show a significant difference when compared to tests without a moving average filter. The results for the shorter 5 and 10 day moving averages are more interesting and show an improvement in annualized ROI. Stocks that are above a long term moving average can have a variety of patterns. They could be basing or pulling back or moving up rapidly. Stocks that are above a short term moving average are more likely moving consistently up. They may be primed for a pullback when the hanging man pattern occurs.

Being above a short term moving average may find patterns similar to the highest day of the last five days' requirement, which was found to improve results as shown in Figure 5.13. When the filters for highest high in the last five days and above the five day simple moving average were combined and used together, the results were not significantly different than those of Figure 5.13. This is another example of how traders should not look to combine a bunch of filters that improve results. Filters interact and overlap and each combination should be tested on its own.

HANGING MAN PATTERN SUMMARY

After examining our results, the research presented here indicates that the results of the hanging man pattern may be improved by: trading the pattern in bearish markets and requiring the pattern to occur as the highest high of the last five days. Even with these improvements the hanging man pattern was not as effective as other tools. As we've learned here, some patterns are good tools to use and some are best left alone.

My research also indicates that results are not improved, or may be diminished, when using the hanging man pattern in the following conditions: requiring volume to be larger than the previous day or larger than average, trading stocks above $20, restricting trades to either high or low volume stocks, requiring the pattern to be the largest range in the last five days, having stock down the day after the pattern, and trading stocks below their 200 day simple moving average.

The improved hanging man pattern requirements are:

- The stock must be in an uptrend.
- The NASDAQ must be in a downtrend or bearish environment.
- The lower shadow must be at least twice the length of the body.
- The body may be either black or white.
- The pattern should occur as the highest high of the last five days.

-CHAPTER 6-

MORNING STAR PATTERNS

I n previous chapters, we have examined the hammer and hanging man candlestick patterns that form in a single bar, and the bullish and bearish engulfing patterns that form in two bars. Now it's time to examine the next level of candlestick patterns.

The morning star pattern is a three bar pattern that marks the end, or reversal, of a downtrend. The first bar is a long black body that indicates a continuation of the downtrend. The second bar features a small body that can be either black or white and gaps lower. The third day of the pattern shows a white body that closes well within the area of the first day's black body.

Figure 6.1 shows an example of a morning star pattern that occurred in LVS on 06/28/07. The first day of the pattern is a large black-bodied candlestick and is marked by the down arrow. The second day of the pattern is a white body that gaps down. The third day completes the morning star pattern by forming a white body that moves well into the area of the first day of the pattern. This morning star pattern marks the end of the LVS downtrend, and the stock bounces 8% in a few days.

Courtesy of AIQ

The second day of the pattern can be either a black or white body. The requirements that the second day gap down and that the body of the candlestick be small are important. Figure 6.2 shows a morning star that formed in SYMM on 03/19/07. The stock was in a downtrend and the first day of the three day pattern was a large black body as marked by the up arrow. On the following day, SYMM gapped down and formed a black body. The pattern was completed on the third day, marked by the down arrow, when the stock moved up and formed a white body that closed well into the area of the first day of the pattern. Following the formation of the morning star pattern, SYMM moved up more than 6% in the next few days.

Morning star patterns are fairly easy to recognize, but the basic definition leaves several parameters open to interpretation. Without a clear definition of what constitutes a "large black body" for the first day of the pattern,

FIGURE 6.2:
MORNING STAR PATTERN IN SYMM ON 03/19/07

Courtesy of AIQ

or a "small body" for the second day of the pattern, or how far into the first day's range the final day of the pattern most close, different traders will pick different patterns. If changes in these parameters do not yield different results, then it does not matter. If slight changes in the parameters affect the trading results, then traders using the morning star should be aware of them.

STANDARD DEFINITION ASSUMPTIONS

Backtesting provides a way for traders to better understand how variations in the definition of the morning star pattern affect trading results. As a starting place for this analysis, I tested the morning star pattern in the period between 01/03/06 and 05/01/07 using the following definitions:

- The first day's "big black bar" must have a body greater than 50% of the day's range.
- The second day's gap down is defined as the opening value on the second day being less than the close of the first day.
- The second day's body must be less than half the day's range.
- The third day's white body must close in the upper half of the first day's range.

The positions were entered at the open on the day following the formation of the morning star pattern, held for five days, then closed. Using these parameters resulted in more than 51% winning trades and a fractional annualized ROI for the 1,476 trades during the period, as shown in Figure 6.3.

Table 6.1 shows the results of investigating the effects of variations in the relationship of the first day's black body to the day's range. The first column

FIGURE 6.3:
INITIAL MORNING STAR TEST RESULTS FOR 01/03/06 TO 05/01/07

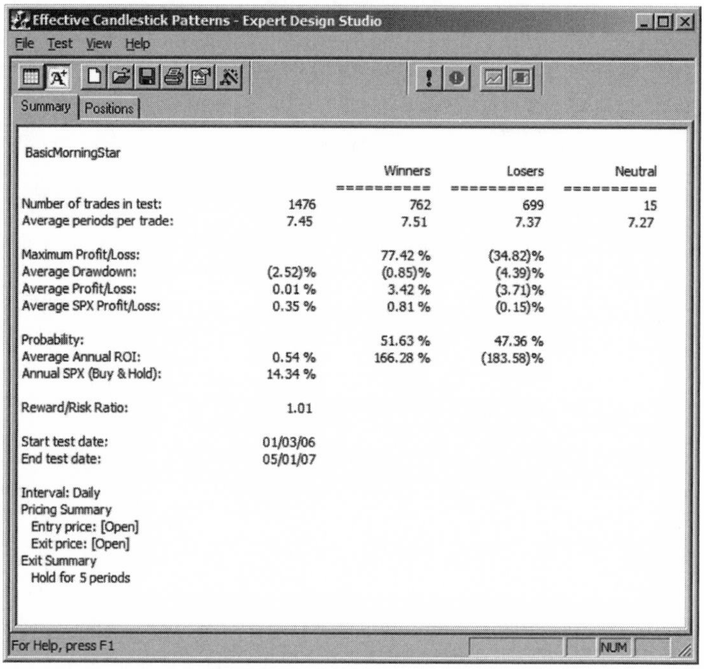

Effective Candlestick Patterns - Expert Design Studio
File Test View Help
Summary Positions
BasicMorningStar

		Winners	Losers	Neutral
Number of trades in test:	1476	762	699	15
Average periods per trade:	7.45	7.51	7.37	7.27
Maximum Profit/Loss:		77.42 %	(34.82)%	
Average Drawdown:	(2.52)%	(0.85)%	(4.39)%	
Average Profit/Loss:	0.01 %	3.42 %	(3.71)%	
Average SPX Profit/Loss:	0.35 %	0.81 %	(0.15)%	
Probability:		51.63 %	47.36 %	
Average Annual ROI:	0.54 %	166.28 %	(183.58)%	
Annual SPX (Buy & Hold):	14.34 %			
Reward/Risk Ratio:	1.01			
Start test date:	01/03/06			
End test date:	05/01/07			

Interval: Daily
Pricing Summary
Entry price: [Open]
Exit price: [Open]
Exit Summary
Hold for 5 periods
For Help, press F1
NUM

Courtesy of AIQ

shows the minimum percentage of the day's range the body must be on the first day of the morning star pattern. The second and third columns show the test results for annualized ROI and percentage of winning trades.

TABLE 6.1
EFFECT OF FIRST DAY BODY SIZE
ON 01/03/06 TO 05/01/07 TEST RESULTS

BODY > PCNT. OF RANGE	ANNUALIZED ROI	WINNING PERCENT
20%	11.81%	52.64%
30%	7.82%	52.44%
40%	6.34%	52.20%
50%	0.54%	51.63%
60%	-8.97%	49.68%

The results shown in Table 6.1 are interesting in that they show improving annualized ROI numbers as smaller and smaller body sizes are allowed when the body size is measured as a percentage of the day's range. In fact, when the requirement of the first day's black body is changed to require it to be less than 30% of the day's trading range, the test results for the period improve significantly, as shown in Figure 6.4. The 23% annualized ROI beats the 14% buy and hold and the percentage of winning trades increases to more than 54%.

An example of the morning star pattern using this small body requirement of the first day of the formation is shown in Figure 6.5. HEB was in a clear downtrend when it formed a black candlestick on 07/20/06 whose body was less than 30% of the day's range. The next day, HEB gapped down and formed a small-bodied candlestick. The third day completed the morning star pattern by moving up well into the range of the first day of the pattern.

FIGURE 6.4:
TEST RESULTS WHEN FIRST DAY BLACK BODY IS <30% OF THE DAY'S RANGE

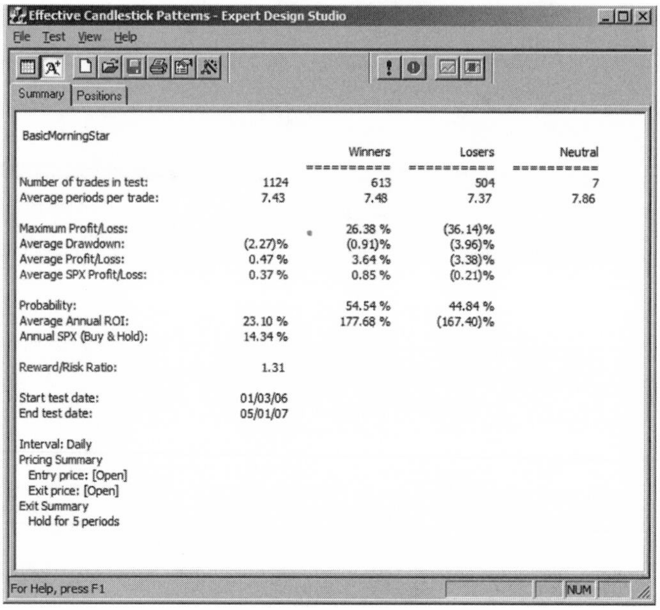
Effective Candlestick Patterns - Expert Design Studio

File Test View Help

Summary | Positions

BasicMorningStar

		Winners	Losers	Neutral
Number of trades in test:	1124	613	504	7
Average periods per trade:	7.43	7.48	7.37	7.86
Maximum Profit/Loss:		26.38 %	(36.14)%	
Average Drawdown:	(2.27)%	(0.91)%	(3.96)%	
Average Profit/Loss:	0.47 %	3.64 %	(3.38)%	
Average SPX Profit/Loss:	0.37 %	0.85 %	(0.21)%	
Probability:		54.54 %	44.84 %	
Average Annual ROI:	23.10 %	177.68 %	(167.40)%	
Annual SPX (Buy & Hold):	14.34 %			
Reward/Risk Ratio:	1.31			
Start test date:	01/03/06			
End test date:	05/01/07			

Interval: Daily
Pricing Summary
Entry price: [Open]
Exit price: [Open]
Exit Summary
Hold for 5 periods

For Help, press F1

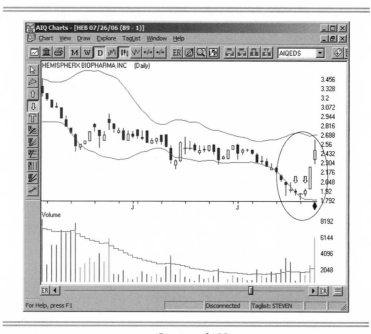

Courtesy of AIQ

FIGURE 6.5:
SMALL FIRST DAY BLACK BODY MORNING STAR IN HEB ON 07/20/06

Courtesy of AIQ

Another example of the small first day morning star pattern is shown in Figure 6.6 in which GMR is in a downtrend and forms a black-bodied candlestick with a body less than 30% of the day's range on 06/12/06, which is followed by a candlestick that gaps down and forms a small body. On the third day of the pattern, GMR moves up and closes well into the range of the first day of the pattern, which completed the morning star.

The small body morning star results outlined above are interesting. Backtesting often leads traders in new and sometimes unexpected directions, which is another reason for going through the process. These results are something worth looking into further, but they also deviate from the typical morning star pattern with which most traders are familiar. That means it's time to investigate other ways to improve the trading results of the more typical pattern.

FIGURE 6.6:
SMALL FIRST DAY BLACK
BODY MORNING STAR IN GMR ON 06/14/06

Courtesy of AIQ

A CLOSER EXAMINATION OF BODY SIZE

The tests above defined the "large body" of the pattern's first day in terms of the range of that day. Another way to define large is in terms of the previous day or days. If the body on the first day of the pattern is required to be larger than the body of the previous day's candlestick, then we will see results as shown in Figure 6.7 for the test period between 01/03/06 and 05/01/07.

Defining the long black body for the first day of the three-day pattern to be larger than the previous day's body yields results that are significantly better than the initial test results. Figure 6.7 indicates that the annualized ROI moves from a fractional gain to more than 10% and the percentage of winning trades also improves.

FIGURE 6.7:
TEST RESULTS FOR MORNING STAR WITH FIRST DAY BODY LARGER THAN PREVIOUS DAY'S BODY

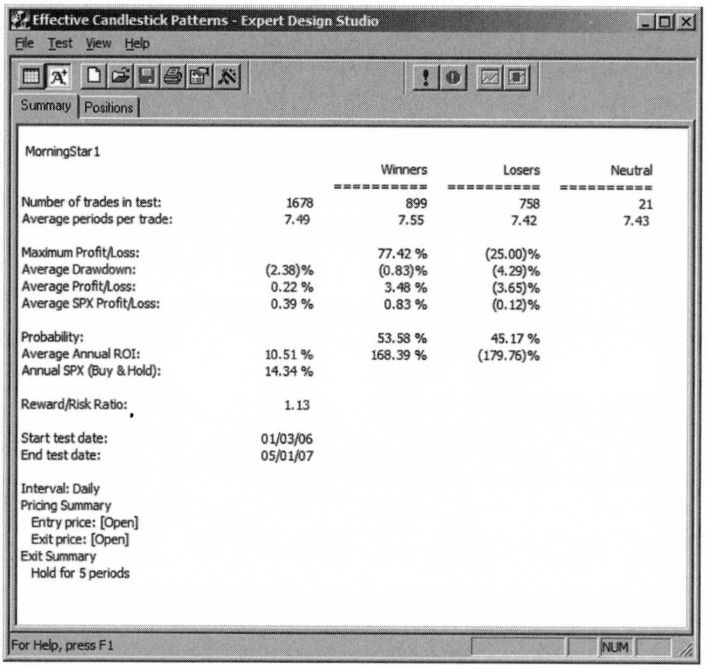

MorningStar1

		Winners	Losers	Neutral
		==========	==========	==========
Number of trades in test:	1678	899	758	21
Average periods per trade:	7.49	7.55	7.42	7.43
Maximum Profit/Loss:		77.42 %	(25.00)%	
Average Drawdown:	(2.38)%	(0.83)%	(4.29)%	
Average Profit/Loss:	0.22 %	3.48 %	(3.65)%	
Average SPX Profit/Loss:	0.39 %	0.83 %	(0.12)%	
Probability:		53.58 %	45.17 %	
Average Annual ROI:	10.51 %	168.39 %	(179.76)%	
Annual SPX (Buy & Hold):	14.34 %			
Reward/Risk Ratio:	1.13			
Start test date:	01/03/06			
End test date:	05/01/07			

Interval: Daily
Pricing Summary
Entry price: [Open]
Exit price: [Open]
Exit Summary
Hold for 5 periods

Courtesy of AIQ

The type of pattern found using this definition of large black body for the first day of the pattern is illustrated in Figure 6.8, in which QSII formed a morning star pattern on 07/28/06. QSII had been in a downtrend, and then on 07/26/06 formed a black-bodied candlestick where the body was larger than the body of the previous day. The next day the stock gapped down and formed a small-bodied candlestick. On the third day the morning star pattern completed when the stock moved up and closed well within the range of the pattern's first day.

When we first looked at the morning star pattern, the definition of "large body" and "small body" was not clearly defined. The test results have indicated that defining the first day's large body as being bigger then the previous day's body improves results, so we will incorporate that into the definition as we

FIGURE 6.8:
LARGE FIRST DAY BODY MORNING STAR IN QSII ON 07/28/06

Courtesy of AIQ

examine other ambiguous parameters of the morning star pattern. As we go through this process, we should end up with a more specific and improved definition of the morning star pattern.

TESTING THE SECOND DAY PARAMETERS

The second day of the morning star pattern has two parameters. It must have a small body, either black or white, and it must gap down. The question arises as to what does "small" mean? Our current definition defines small in terms of a percentage of the day's range. The results of Figure 6.7 were obtained using the original definition that required the body of the second day of the morning star pattern to be less than half the day's range.

Table 6.2 shows the results of testing variations in the maximum percentage the second day's body can be in relation to the range of the second day. The fourth line shows the results for requiring that the body on the second day of the pattern be less than 50% of the second day's range. This is the original definition and is the same as the results shown in Figure 6.7. Requiring smaller body sizes than this on the second day of the pattern reduces results.

Based on this information, I would change the morning star definition to require a second day body size less than 60% of the day's range, unless subsequent testing showed a better alternative.

I also looked at defining a small body on the second day of the morning star pattern in terms of its relationship to the previous day's body size instead of the relationship to the second day's range. After testing several different percentage relationships, I did not find one that significantly improved results. Based on these results, I modified the initial parameters noted above to define the small body on the second day of the pattern as being less than 60% of the second day's range.

TABLE 6.2
EFFECT OF SECOND DAY BODY
SIZE ON 01/03/06 TO 05/01/07 TEST RESULTS

BODY PCNT. OF RANGE	ANNUALIZED ROI	WINNING PERCENT
20%	8.47%	53.48%
30%	4.23%	52.12%
40%	6.23%	52.14%
50%	10.51%	53.58%
60%	12.24%	53.83%
70%	11.65%	53.58%

EXAMINING GAPS

The second parameter for the second day of the morning star pattern is the requirement that the stock gap down. Gaps are a popular topic of conversation among traders; there are lots of ideas and theories about trading gaps. There are some gap trading strategies with promising results, but there is also a lot of folklore that does not seem to pan out.

In this case, the only requirement we have for day two of the morning star pattern is that it gap down. Would the results change if we only looked at patterns in which the close on day two was also below the previous day's close, or if the high of day two was lower than the close of the previous day? Once again testing is the way to find out.

Test results for morning star patterns during this test period that showed a close on day two below the close of the first day of the pattern indicated a slight increase in annualized ROI, but nothing dramatic or conclusive. Taking morning star trades when the close of the second day of the pattern was below the low of the first day of the pattern (the big black bar) was more interesting.

Figure 6.9 shows that during the 01/03/06 to 05/01/07 test period, adding a new requirement to the definition of the second day of the pattern (that its close be below the low of the first day of the pattern) improved the annualized ROI to more than 17%, which is more than the buy and hold annualized ROI. The percentage of winning trades also improved to nearly 57%. This is a requirement worth considering if further testing confirms the results in other time frames.

FIGURE 6.9:
TEST RESULTS FOR MORNING STARS
WITH SECOND DAY CLOSE BELOW THE FIRST DAY'S LOW

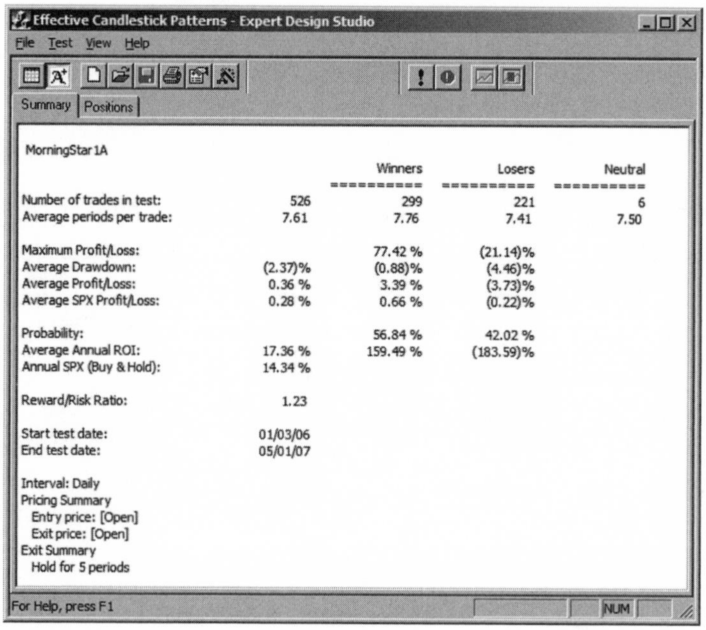

Effective Candlestick Patterns - Expert Design Studio			
File Test View Help			
Summary Positions			
MorningStar 1A			
	Winners	Losers	Neutral
Number of trades in test: 526	299	221	6
Average periods per trade: 7.61	7.76	7.41	7.50
Maximum Profit/Loss:	77.42 %	(21.14)%	
Average Drawdown: (2.37)%	(0.88)%	(4.46)%	
Average Profit/Loss: 0.36 %	3.39 %	(3.73)%	
Average SPX Profit/Loss: 0.28 %	0.66 %	(0.22)%	
Probability:	56.84 %	42.02 %	
Average Annual ROI: 17.36 %	159.49 %	(183.59)%	
Annual SPX (Buy & Hold): 14.34 %			
Reward/Risk Ratio: 1.23			
Start test date: 01/03/06			
End test date: 05/01/07			
Interval: Daily			
Pricing Summary			
Entry price: [Open]			
Exit price: [Open]			
Exit Summary			
Hold for 5 periods			
For Help, press F1		NUM	

Courtesy of AIQ

If we only took trades that show the high on day two of the pattern to be less than the low of the first day, we saw very interesting results, as shown in Figure 6.10. The annualized ROI jumped to more than 52% and the percentage of winning trades dropped to just more than 48%. The annualized ROI was high even with slightly less than a 50% winning trade percentage because the average winning trade returned nearly twice what the average losing trade lost.

Since most traders focus on the annualized ROI number, let's look closer at the results of Figure 6.10. When examining test results, the total number of trades produced during the test period is important. A small number of trades may not be statistically valid or may be caused by some unique event occurring during the test period. One way to determine if this is the case is to test the pattern in a longer period to see if similar results are produced.

FIGURE 6.10:
TEST RESULTS FOR MORNING STARS
WITH SECOND DAY HIGH BELOW THE FIRST DAY'S LOW

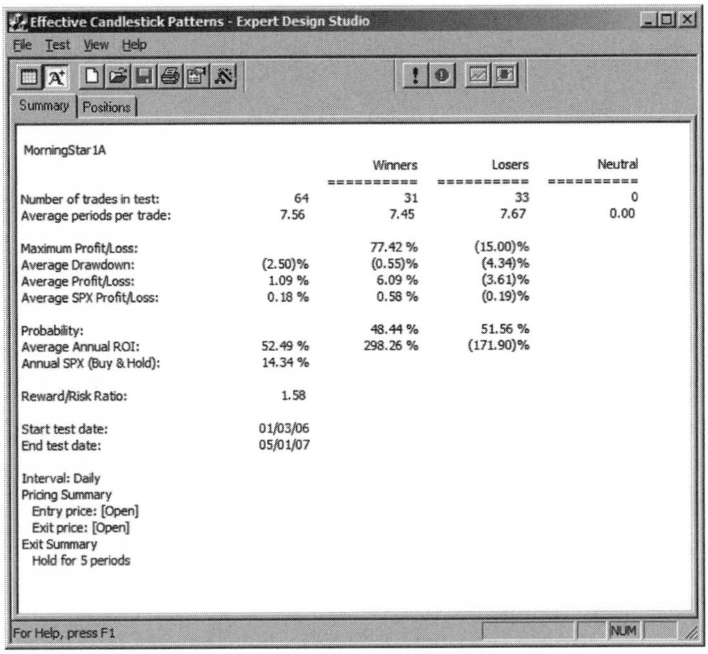

Effective Candlestick Patterns - Expert Design Studio			

File Test View Help

Summary | Positions

MorningStar 1A

		Winners	Losers	Neutral
Number of trades in test:	64	31	33	0
Average periods per trade:	7.56	7.45	7.67	0.00
Maximum Profit/Loss:		77.42 %	(15.00)%	
Average Drawdown:	(2.50)%	(0.55)%	(4.34)%	
Average Profit/Loss:	1.09 %	6.09 %	(3.61)%	
Average SPX Profit/Loss:	0.18 %	0.58 %	(0.19)%	
Probability:		48.44 %	51.56 %	
Average Annual ROI:	52.49 %	298.26 %	(171.90)%	
Annual SPX (Buy & Hold):	14.34 %			
Reward/Risk Ratio:	1.58			
Start test date:	01/03/06			
End test date:	05/01/07			

Interval: Daily
Pricing Summary
  Entry price: [Open]
  Exit price: [Open]
Exit Summary
  Hold for 5 periods

For Help, press F1   NUM

Courtesy of AIQ

This leads to another issue: Some traders feel the longer the test period, the more valid the results. This also has issues, as we shall see.

Running the test in a period more than twice as long, 01/02/04 to 05/01/07, resulted in 124 trades with an annualized ROI of nearly 41% (compared to 10% for buy and hold) and 50% winning trades. This shows that even though the system does not produce hundreds of trades, it does show interesting results in two different time frames.

TESTING A LONGER TIME FRAME

At this point you may be thinking that we should test this version of the morning star pattern in a very long time frame. Testing this during the 7½-year period from the end of 1999 to May of 2007 showed an annualized ROI of negative 25%, and the winning percentage dropped to 42%. What happened? Does the system just fail in longer time frames?

The answer, like many things in trading, comes by looking at the market. Figure 6.11 shows the NASDAQ during the December 1999 to May 2007 test period. During 2000, 2001, and 2002, the market dropped around 80%. As I recall during the first part of that period, the talking heads on the financial shows were encouraging people to "stay the course," "believe in America," and worst of all, "buy the dips." This illustrates how important it is to learn how to read the charts yourself because anyone who knew how to draw trend lines was either out or short in 2000.

The period between 03/31/00 and 10/04/02 was one of the worst bear markets in history, with the NASDAQ declining from the 5,000 area to the 1,100 area. Testing the morning star pattern during this period (with the requirement that the second day's high be below the first day's low) showed 130 trades and an annualized loss of 111%. Only 32% of the trades were profitable. This pattern, and many other long systems, was not able to overcome the strong bearish tendencies of the market during this unique period.

From 10/24/02 to 05/01/07, the market showed a number of normal up and down cycles, but nothing as dramatic as the 2000 to 2002 period. Between 10/24/02 and 05/01/07, this modified morning star pattern showed 142 trades, a little less than three a month, and an annualized ROI of 46%. Winning trades returned an average of 5.3% and losing trades lost an average of 3.6%.

The key point here is to show that market conditions have a strong effect on most trading patterns, and it is important for traders to understand how their patterns perform in different market conditions. It is also important to understand that testing in a longer time frame does not necessarily produce more reliable results. Some traders feel that if a two-year test is good, a five-year test must be more accurate, and an eight-year test would be even better for accurately representing how a pattern performs. Sometimes this is not the case because unusual market conditions can overpower the results.

As we have seen here, increasing the test period length from two to five years might lead one to believe the trading pattern is solid. Another trader who only tested the pattern in the eight year period from 2000 to 2007 would see negative results and conclude the pattern is not worth trading. The difference is that the eight-year period includes one of the worst bear markets in history.

FIGURE 6.11:
NASDAQ MARKET BETWEEN DEC. 1999 AND MAY 2007

Courtesy of AIQ

What are the odds of the market showing another eight-year period like that in the near future? Not likely. This is why just arbitrarily increasing the test period does not ensure more accurate results when testing trading patterns. Traders can get a better idea of how a system performs by testing in multiple instances of all three basic market conditions.

The Issue of Statistical Relevance

An interesting issue raised by these test results is how to deal with trading patterns that end in a low number of trades during the test period. The heart of this issue is whether the test results are statistically significant. In this case, we saw similar results in two different testing periods, which indicated the filter may not be curve fitting the data in one time frame. However, we should be on our guard when we see a small number of trades during a long test period. It raises some questions as to how likely the results are to be replicated in the future.

A more practical question is that trading less than three patterns a month may not provide enough opportunity for profit. Making a trade every couple of weeks and annualizing the results can give a good annualized ROI, but total dollars flowing into the trader's account may not be as strong as a pattern with a lower annualized ROI and more consistent trades. Typically, I want to see trading patterns that provide multiple opportunities every week. Because of this issue, I will go back to the requirement of the second day's close being below the first day's low. The results of using this requirement are shown in Figure 6.9.

DOES BODY COLOR MATTER?

In the process of making the morning star pattern more specific, we have analyzed the effects of changing the parameters of body size and of a gap down on the second day. The last aspect of the second day of the pattern is the assertion that the body color does not matter. Let's test that assertion.

The data in Figure 6.12 indicates that during the 01/03/06 to 05/01/07 test period, trading morning star patterns with black bodies on the second day improved both the annualized ROI and the percentage of winning trades as compared to the results of Figure 6.9, which allowed second day black bodies of either color. An example morning star pattern with a black body on the second day of the pattern is shown in Figure 6.13.

FIGURE 6.12:
**TEST RESULTS FOR MORNING
STARS WITH SECOND DAY BLACK BODIES**

Effective Candlestick Patterns - Expert Design Studio

File Test View Help

Summary | Positions |

MorningStar 1A

		Winners	Losers	Neutral
Number of trades in test:	419	247	167	5
Average periods per trade:	7.53	7.65	7.38	7.00
Maximum Profit/Loss:		77.42 %	(21.14)%	
Average Drawdown:	(2.34)%	(0.90)%	(4.54)%	
Average Profit/Loss:	0.61 %	3.58 %	(3.77)%	
Average SPX Profit/Loss:	0.29 %	0.61 %	(0.18)%	
Probability:		58.95 %	39.86 %	
Average Annual ROI:	29.57 %	170.96 %	(186.39)%	
Annual SPX (Buy & Hold):	14.34 %			
Reward/Risk Ratio:	1.41			
Start test date:	01/03/06			
End test date:	05/01/07			

Interval: Daily
Pricing Summary
  Entry price: [Open]
  Exit price: [Open]
Exit Summary
  Hold for 5 periods

For Help, press F1   NUM

Courtesy of AIQ

MORNING STAR WITH SECOND DAY BLACK BODY

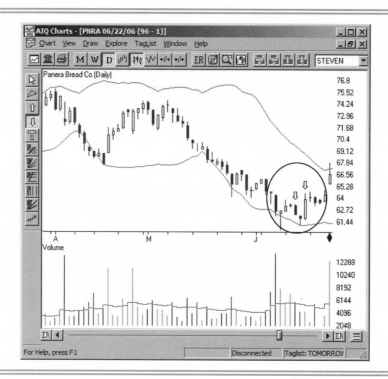

Courtesy of AIQ

Testing the requirement of the second day black body in the longer time frame of 01/02/04 to 05/01/07 resulted in a 29% annualized ROI (10% for buy and hold) and a winning percentage of nearly 55% percent. This is an improvement over the 20% annualized ROI and 54% winning trades that resulted during the same period when taking trades of either body color on the second day of the pattern.

During these two test periods, the results favor taking morning star trades with black bodies on the second day of the pattern. I also tested the effect of only taking trades during the 01/02/04 to 05/01/07 test period with white bodies on the second day. The test results shown in Figure 6.14 indicate that taking morning star trades with white second day bodies during the 01/02/04 to 05/01/07 period results in a small annualized ROI loss. Testing the second day black bodies in multiple time frames showed an improvement in results, and testing second day white bodies showed a decrease in results. Based on

```
Effective Candlestick Patterns - Expert Design Studio                    _ □ ×
File  Test  View  Help

□ A'  □ ☞ 🖫 ☕ 🖻 🖎              ! 0 🖾 🔳
Summary | Positions |

MorningStar 1A
                                      Winners      Losers      Neutral
                                    ==========  ==========  ==========
Number of trades in test:       217     117           98            2
Average periods per trade:     7.43     7.59         7.22         8.50

Maximum Profit/Loss:                   20.15 %     (20.56)%
Average Drawdown:            (2.37)%    (0.66)%     (4.46)%
Average Profit/Loss:         (0.02)%     2.94 %     (3.55)%
Average SPX Profit/Loss:      0.34 %     0.88 %     (0.31)%

Probability:                           53.92 %     45.16 %
Average Annual ROI:          (0.85)%   141.34 %   (179.21)%
Annual SPX (Buy & Hold):     10.09 %

Reward/Risk Ratio:            0.99

Start test date:            01/02/04
End test date:              05/01/07

Interval: Daily
Pricing Summary
  Entry price: [Open]
  Exit price: [Open]
Exit Summary
  Hold for 5 periods

For Help, press F1                                          NUM
```

Courtesy of AIQ

these results, I will incorporate the requirement for a second day black body into the morning star definition.

THIRD DAY PARAMETERS

The requirements for the third day of the morning star pattern are relatively simple. It must be a white body and it must close within the top half of the range of the first day of the pattern. I tested different requirements for how far into the first day's range the last day must close and did not find anything that significantly helped the results.

Gaps may indicate strength, so I tested a requirement that the last day of the pattern gap up. During the 01/03/06 to 05/10/07 test period, this new requirement resulted in a slight decrease in the annualized ROI and the percentage of winning trades. Therefore, a gap up on the third day of the pattern does not appear to be something worth incorporating into the morning star definition.

I also found that during this test period, requiring the third day of the pattern to have the largest range of the last five days did not help results. This requirement was found to be useful in other patterns, but does not help the morning star pattern.

EXIT STRATEGIES—TESTING THE HOLDING PERIOD

All of the testing to this point has used a five day holding period as the exit strategy. The stock was purchased at the open on the day after the morning star pattern appeared and held for five days then sold. The morning star pattern was tested using during 01/03/06 to 05/01/07 using different holding periods as shown in Table 6.3.

TABLE 6.3
MORNING STAR TEST RESULTS WITH DIFFERENT HOLDING PERIODS

Holding Period	Annualized ROI	Winning Percent
7 Days	17.13%	50.24%
6 Days	18.06%	52.15%
5 Days	29.57%	58.95%
4 Days	40.97%	57.01%
3 Days	25.27%	53.21%

Table 6.3 indicates that a four day holding period seems to perform the best. As a practical matter, I use this information as a guideline when trading patterns. I would not automatically sell after four days, but instead watch the market environment, the price/volume pattern of the stock, and support/resistance areas for guidance on when to exit.

If the market takes a sudden move down on big volume or breaks a support area, I will look at closing positions whether or not it has been four days. If the stock runs into a key resistance area, I will take profits early. If the stock is moving up on declining volume, I will take profits early. I may also hold longer than four days if the market is in a strong move or the stock is moving up on strong volume. I use test results as a guideline, not an absolute trading system. Experience and market knowledge count for a lot. When in doubt, I take profits. It is hard to go broke taking profits.

Using this definition of the pattern and testing it with a four day holding period in multiple time frames produced the results shown in Table 6.4. In six different time frames from 1½ to more than 10 years, this modified morning star definition had an annualized ROI significantly better than buy and hold and a winning trade percentage in the mid '50s.

Does this testing imply that you will win on 55% of your morning star trades and be profitable in any given time period? No. It does indicate the pattern has performed well in the past and provides a reasonable basis for thinking it may continue to do so in the future if the market conditions are similar to the last few years.

Remember that if you win 50% of the time, it does not mean every other trade will be profitable. Traders can and do see consecutive losing streaks for 8 or 10 trades in a row and need to adjust their risk profile to allow for this. If you flip a coin 10 times, you would expect that you would get 5 heads and 5 tails, and if you do the experiment a large number of times, you should see something close to half heads and half tails.

There is a 1-in-1,024 chance that flipping a coin 10 times will come up heads every time. The odds of that happening are not great, but it is possible. In fact, if you do the experiment 2,000 times, there is a reasonably good chance you will see it happen once. If you are an active trader and make a thousand trades over a few years, you also have a pretty good chance of seeing 10 losing trades in a row at some point. This is why experienced traders adjust the amount they are risking on each trade to allow for this eventuality.

TABLE 6.4
MORNING STAR TEST RESULTS IN DIFFERENT TIME PERIODS

Test Period	Annualized ROI	Buy & Hold ROI	Winning Percent
01/03/06 to 05/01/07	40.97%	14.34%	57.01%
01/03/05 to 05/01/07	32.21%	9.72%	53.79%
01/03/04 to 05/01/07	38.69%	10.09%	55.31%
01/03/03 to 05/01/07	38.74%	15.90%	54.65%
01/03/02 to 05/01/07	33.38%	5.52%	53.74%
01/03/97 to 05/01/07	45.21%	9.73%	53.34%

MORNING STAR PATTERN SUMMARY

After examining thousands of morning star patterns in different market conditions and using various filters, the test results presented above indicate that trading the morning star pattern may be improved if traders consider trading patterns where the first day's body size is less than 30% of the first days trading range. Trading results may also be improved by trading patterns where the first day's black body is larger than the previous day's body, or requiring the second day's body to be less than 60% of the second day's range, or requiring the close of the second day of the pattern to be below the low of the first day of the pattern. Test results are also improved when the second day of the pattern has a black, rather than white, body; and when using a 4 to 5 day holding period.

The testing also indicates that results are not improved, or may be diminished, when using morning star patterns that have a body on the second day of the pattern that is smaller than the body on the first day of the pattern, or when the third day of the pattern starts with a gap up, or when using a holding period less than four days or more than five days.

A large range on the third day of the pattern does not seem to help results nor is there a strong correlation between test results and how far into the upper half of the first day's range the close on the third day of the pattern is. It is just important that the third day of the pattern closes at a price level somewhere in the upper half of the first day's range.

Requiring that the close on day two is lower than the close on day one of the pattern does not significantly improve testing results. Note that requiring the close on day two of the pattern to be lower than the low of day one improves results, but just requiring the low of day two to be lower than the close of day one does not significantly improve results.

The improved morning star pattern requirements are:
• The stock must be in a downtrend.
• The first day of the pattern must be:
    ~ A black bar.
    ~ Have a body larger than the previous day's body.
• The second day of the pattern must:
    ~ Open below the close of the first day.
    ~ Have a body less than 60% of the day's range.
    ~ Be a black body.
• The third day of the pattern must:
    ~ Be a white body.
    ~ Must close above the middle of the first day's range.

CHAPTER 7

EVENING STAR PATTERNS

T he evening star is a three bar reversal pattern that may signal the end of a stock's uptrend. The first candlestick in the pattern has a long white body, indicating the current uptrend is continuing. The second candlestick gaps up and then forms a small body. It is as if the enthusiasm of the initial opening gap up cannot be maintained, and the distance between the open and close is not very large. The third candle is a black candle, indicating a reversal of sentiment; the black candle must close at least halfway down the range of the first day's candlestick.

Figure 7.1 shows an evening star pattern in DIA. The stock was in an uptrend and showed a long white body on 05/09/06. The following day DIA gapped up and formed a small body, which was followed by a large black body on 05/11/06 to complete the pattern. After the formation of the evening star pattern, DIA dropped about five points during the next few days.

Figure 7.2 shows another evening star pattern that occurred in MDG on 02/23/07. MDG had been in an uptrend and formed a large white body on 02/21/07, which was followed by a gap up the following day and the

FIGURE 7.1:
EVENING STAR PATTERN IN DIA

Courtesy of AIQ

formation of a small black body. On the third and final day of the pattern, MDG formed a large black body which marked an end to the recent uptrend, and the stock dropped nearly 11% during the next four days.

The definition of the evening star leaves some room for interpretation, and different traders may not classify some patterns as evening stars. For example, the definition of the third day of the pattern requires the candle to close at least halfway down the range of the first day. If the third day gapped down well below the low of the first day, it would still meet this definition, yet some traders would not look at the resulting pattern and call it an evening star.

Some of the literature on evening stars requires a gap between the first and second days of the pattern and also a gap between the second and third days of the pattern. As we've seen with the other patterns, variations among

Courtesy of AIQ

the definitions and some uncertainty of the adjectives sometimes make it difficult for new traders to understand exactly what to look for. Backtesting not only gives us an idea of what one might expect in trading the pattern, it also gives us a tool for exploring how different variations in the parameters of the pattern's definition affect the results. Using this technique allows us to test different definitions and select the one(s) that seem to work best.

INITIAL TEST ON THE STANDARD ELEMENTS

In order to backtest the evening star pattern, I started with the definition below and used a four-day holding period. The initial test period was 01/03/06 to 05/01/07. After a pattern formed that met the definition below, a short position was entered at the open the following day and held for four days before being closed.

• The stock must be in an uptrend.

• Day one requires:

~ A white body.

~ A body larger than the previous day's body.

• Day two requires:

~ Either color body.

~ A body less than 60% of the previous day's body.

~ A gap up, defined as the opening being above the previous day's close.

• Day three requires:

~ A black body.

~ A close below the midpoint of the range of day one.

FIGURE 7.3:
EVENING STAR TEST RESULTS DURING 01/03/06 TO 05/01/07

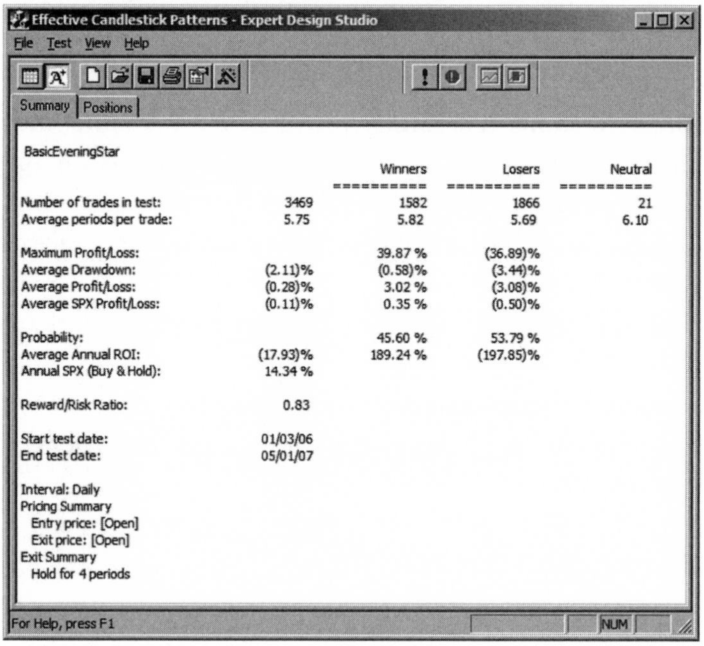

BasicEveningStar		Winners	Losers	Neutral
Number of trades in test:	3469	1582	1866	21
Average periods per trade:	5.75	5.82	5.69	6.10
Maximum Profit/Loss:		39.87 %	(36.89)%	
Average Drawdown:	(2.11)%	(0.58)%	(3.44)%	
Average Profit/Loss:	(0.28)%	3.02 %	(3.08)%	
Average SPX Profit/Loss:	(0.11)%	0.35 %	(0.50)%	
Probability:		45.60 %	53.79 %	
Average Annual ROI:	(17.93)%	189.24 %	(197.85)%	
Annual SPX (Buy & Hold):	14.34 %			
Reward/Risk Ratio:	0.83			
Start test date:	01/03/06			
End test date:	05/01/07			

Interval: Daily
Pricing Summary
  Entry price: [Open]
  Exit price: [Open]
Exit Summary
  Hold for 4 periods

Courtesy of AIQ

The initial test results were a little surprising, as shown in Figure 7.3. Taking all of the evening star trades during the test period showed an annualized ROI with an 18% loss, and less than 46% of the trades were winners. Not exactly an inspiring start; but trading is about knowing what is, not about hoping what might be. Whether or not a trading pattern or a filter works, we learn something by knowing what it does, and in the trading business knowledge can make you money and keep you out of trouble.

Testing the initial evening star pattern in the longer time frame of 01/02/04 to 05/01/07 yielded about the same results, so it is possible that the poor return is due to the pattern itself and not just a function of one specific time frame. We can use backtesting techniques to investigate the affects of changing parameters of each day of the three day evening star pattern.

TESTING THE THIRD DAY

If you remember, the first step we took to gain a better understanding of the morning star pattern was to look at the results of testing the pattern with several variations of the definition in the requirements for the third day. Using that as our starting point, I reviewed a number of the initial testing charts and noticed many of the evening star patterns had third days much lower than the first day of the pattern. I call these "low3" and an example is shown in Figure 7.4.

LOW3 TEST

Figure 7.4 shows that TNH was in an uptrend and formed a large white body on 04/05, followed by a gap up with a small body, which then was followed by a black body that closed below the midpoint of the first day of the pattern. It is a low3 because the third day of this pattern closed well below the first day of the pattern, which is within the definition of most evening stars but not the type of example that is shown in most texts.

Since the low3 style of evening star looks different than what is usually shown for a evening star pattern, I tested to see what the effect would be

Courtesy of AIQ

of requiring that day three have a close greater than the low of the first day of the pattern. This requirement resulted in patterns that looked more like what you often see in books and magazines, but it actually hurt the annualized ROI numbers. It appears better to allow the bar of the third day of the pattern to extend below the bar of the first day.

Results can be improved by requiring that the third day of the pattern have a body length that is the largest body length in the last five days. An example of this type of pattern is shown in Figure 7.5, where TIE showed an evening star with a long body on the third day of the pattern. During the next few days after the evening star formed, TIE dropped about 17%, leading to a nice profit for short positions.

Taking only long-bodied evening stars during the 01/03/06 to 05/01/07 test period resulted in improved annualized ROI and the percentage of winning

FIGURE 7.5:
LONG DAY 3 BODY EVENING STAR IN TIE ON 05/12/06

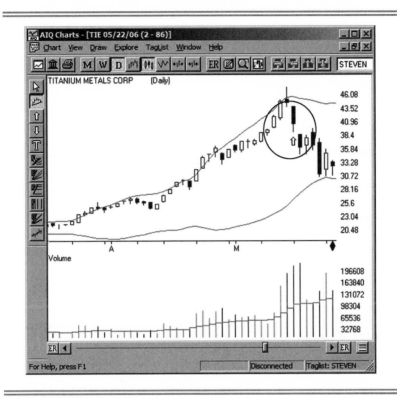

Courtesy of AIQ

trades. This variation in the requirements for the third day of the evening star pattern did not improve results enough to beat buy and hold, but perhaps when combined with other parameter changes, this could result in a more interesting trading pattern.

GAPS

A number of traders feel the evening star pattern is stronger if the third day of the three day pattern opens with a gap down. Adding a filter requiring the open on the third to be less than the close of the second day of the pattern resulted in a small increase in ROI from negative 18% to negative 15.7%, and left the winning trade percentage about the same. Neither of these results is significant enough to warrant changing the basic pattern parameters of the evening star trading pattern.

The gap tested is a basic gap in which the open is lower than the previous day's close. This type of gap is relatively common, and, as we have seen, is not helpful in terms of improving the trading results of the evening star pattern. When the gap is larger and the high falls below the low of the previous day's trading, it forms a "white space" on the chart and is much more visible than the typical gap. An example of a "white space gap" is shown in Figure 7.6.

In Figure 7.6, BTU has been in an uptrend and forms an evening star pattern, which completes on 02/07/06. The third day of the evening star pattern starts with a strong gap down, and BTU opens below the close of the previous

FIGURE 7.6:
WHITE SPACE GAP ON DAY 3 OF
EVENING STAR IN BTU ON 02/07/06

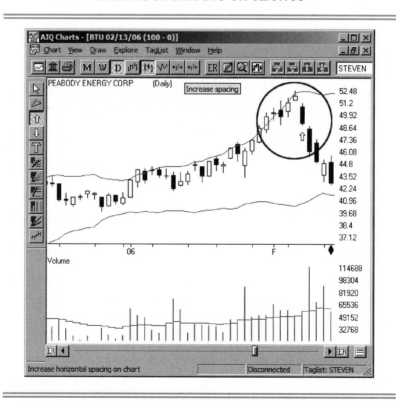

Courtesy of AIQ

TEST RESULTS FOR WHITE SPACE GAP ON DAY 3 EVENING STARS

Courtesy of AIQ

day. When a stock opens below the previous day's low, it results in a "white space gap."

Only taking evening star patterns with white space gaps on the third day of the pattern during the 01/03/06 to 05/01/07 test period, results in 312 trades showing an annualized ROI of slightly less than 8%; and more than 51% winning trades as shown in Figure 7.7. These results are not strong enough to use the pattern for trading, but do indicate the power of white space gaps of the third day since this is the first parameter change that has resulted in a positive annualized ROI.

TESTING THE SECOND DAY

WHITE SPACE GAPS

One might think that if a white space gap on day three of the pattern helped the trading results more than anything else so far, then perhaps using a white space gap on day two instead of just a simple gap would also improve results. Figure 7.8 shows the test results for trading only evening star patterns with white space gaps on day two of the pattern. This parameter change resulted in significantly fewer trades and a larger annualized ROI loss than the basic definition with which we started. Our testing showed that white space gaps improve results when they occur on day three of the pattern and reduce results when they occur on day two of the pattern.

FIGURE 7.8:
TEST RESULTS FOR WHITE SPACE GAP ON DAY 2 EVENING STARS

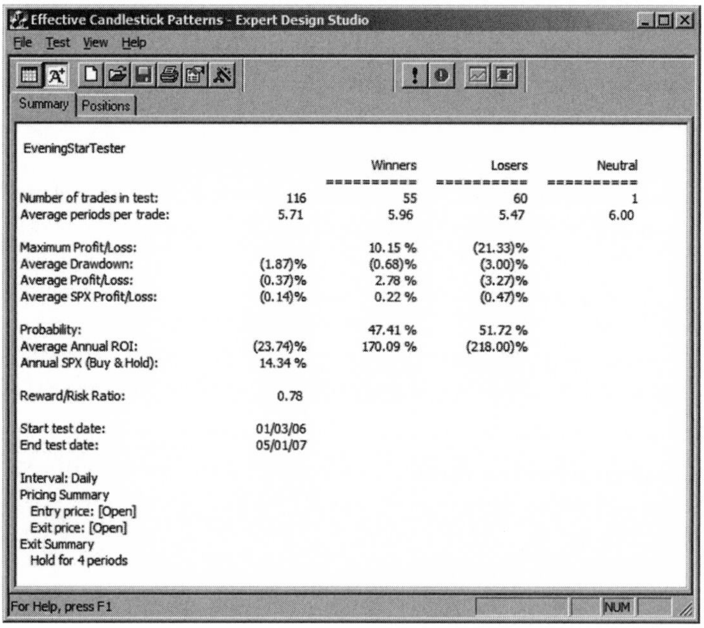

Effective Candlestick Patterns - Expert Design Studio

File Test View Help

Summary Positions

EveningStarTester

		Winners	Losers	Neutral
Number of trades in test:	116	55	60	1
Average periods per trade:	5.71	5.96	5.47	6.00
Maximum Profit/Loss:		10.15 %	(21.33)%	
Average Drawdown:	(1.87)%	(0.68)%	(3.00)%	
Average Profit/Loss:	(0.37)%	2.78 %	(3.27)%	
Average SPX Profit/Loss:	(0.14)%	0.22 %	(0.47)%	
Probability:		47.41 %	51.72 %	
Average Annual ROI:	(23.74)%	170.09 %	(218.00)%	
Annual SPX (Buy & Hold):	14.34 %			
Reward/Risk Ratio:	0.78			
Start test date:	01/03/06			
End test date:	05/01/07			

Interval: Daily
Pricing Summary
Entry price: [Open]
Exit price: [Open]
Exit Summary
Hold for 4 periods

For Help, press F1

Courtesy of AIQ

If the requirement that day two of the pattern show a gap up is eliminated, the test results were similar to the initial evening star test results shown in Figure 7.3, with the exception that, as expected, a lot more trades occured. In this particular test period, it appears a gap on the third day of the pattern is more important than a gap on the first day, and a white space gap on the third day is more powerful that just a simple gap.

In addition to the requirement for a gap up, the basic definition of the evening star pattern requires a small body on day two, and allows it to be either black or white. Testing the performance of the evening star pattern with variations in these parameters will help us to understand how important they are.

BODY SIZE

Most of the literature on evening star patterns does not attach a specific definition to "small" body size on day two of the pattern. The basic definition for a small body on day two used for the results in Figure 7.3 was the body size must be less than 60% of the day one body size. Table 7.1 indicated the test results were similar for body sizes 40% or more of the first day's body size. The results made an obvious improvement when the requirement was changed to 30% or less.

Remember, there are a number of different issues that can cause effects in backtesting results. This is why I am not interested in changing a parameter unless there is a clear difference in using it. In the first five lines of Table 7.1, the annualized ROI results only vary by about 4%. The effects of time frames, database quality, slippage, etc., can also account for a few percentage points difference. When the body size for day two drops to 30% or less of the day one body size, the annualized ROI loss is halved; that kind of result is something worth listening to.

TABLE 7.1
EFFECT OF DAY 2 BODY SIZE ON
EVENING STAR TEST RESULTS 01/03/06 TO 05/01/07

DAY 2 BODY % OF DAY1	ANNUALIZED ROI	WINNING PERCENT
80%	-17.88%	45.50%
70%	-17.20%	45.44%
60%	-17.93%	45.60%
50%	-15.06%	46.17%
40%	-13.05%	45.92%
30%	-7.91%	46.51%
20%	-7.92%	46.88%

Since changing the definition of "small body" on day two of the pattern to less than 30% of the day one body size cuts the annualized ROI loss in half and still results in over 1,700 trades during the 01/03/06 to 05/01/07 test period, I will be incorporating this into the standard definition and using it in subsequent tests. I have not yet incorporated the requirement for a day three white space gap down into the definition because it significantly reduced the number of trades.

BODY COLOR

The other parameter of the second day is that the body color does not matter; it can be either black or white. This idea was tested by adding a filter to the evening star definition that resulted in only taking trades when the body on the second day of the pattern was white. The results were interesting because the annualized ROI loss dropped from minus 18% to slightly under minus 6%. This effect also held up when testing in the longer time frame of 01/02/04 to 05/01/07.

I noticed an interesting effect when testing white body candlesticks on day two of the pattern that may affect some traders. When charting programs draw candlesticks, the horizontal lines used to draw the top and bottom of the candlestick body have a width. Because of the width of these lines, some very small body candlestick patterns appear to be black body candlesticks due to the very small amount of white space in the body of the candlestick. This is something worth keeping in mind.

As an example, Figure 7.9 shows an evening star pattern that occurred in ESL on 05/08/06, where the third day of the pattern is marked by an up arrow. The second day appears to be a black body in the chart. Closer inspection reveals that the open was 45.88 and the close was 46.28, indicating the stock had an up day and a white candlestick. The candlestick just appears to be black because the white space between the open and close is small compared to the line width used to draw the top and bottom parts of the candlestick

FIGURE 7.9:
EVENING STAR IN ESL ON 05/08/06

Courtesy of AIQ

body. This should not be an issue when using a computer scan to find the pattern, but it can lead traders to skip over some white-bodied candlesticks when visually scanning charts.

TESTING THE FIRST DAY—WHAT IS BIG?

The first day of the evening star pattern has the simplest definition; it just has to be a "big" black candlestick. The definition of a black candlestick is unambiguous. The definition of "big" leaves room for traders to interpret the word differently and thus trade different patterns. In order to get a better idea of what definition to use, the test was run several times using various definitions for "big," with the results listed in Table 7.2.

To get the results for Table 7.2, the test was run six times during 01/03/06 to 05/01/07. The first line shows the results for taking all evening star trades during the period when the first day had a larger body than the previous day. The second line shows the results for evening star patterns whose first day body was larger than the bodies on the two previous days and so on to the last line, where the first day of the evening star pattern was required to have a body larger than any of the previous six days.

The third line in Table 7.2 has the best results, and in fact turns a losing system into a winning percentage. The 3½% gain is still below the 14% annualized ROI for buy and hold, so this is not yet a pattern I would focus on trading, but we are definitely beginning to understand how to define the different parameters in the pattern.

Based on the results of Table 7.2, I altered the parameters of the first day of the evening star pattern to require that the black body of the first day be larger than any body of the three previous candlesticks. An example of what this looks like is shown in Figure 7.10, in which an evening star pattern appeared in RGLD on 12/29/06. Note that the body on the first day of the three day pattern was the largest body in the last three days.

TABLE 7.2
EFFECT OF DAY 1 BODY SIZE ON
EVENING STAR TEST RESULTS 01/03/06 TO 05/01/07

DAY 1 BODY BIGGEST IN X DAYS	ANNUALIZED ROI	WINNING PERCENT
1	-7.91%	46.51%
2	-3.45%	47.53%
3	3.50%	48.93%
4	0.55%	49.28%
5	-3.65%	48.70%
6	-3.74%	48.15%

FIGURE 7.10:
THREE DAY WIDE RANGE EVENING STAR IN RGLD ON 12/29/06

Courtesy of AIQ

ANALYZING THE RESULTS

The testing of the evening star pattern to this point has indicated it performs better when two modifications are made to the basic definition. These are 1)the body of the first day is the largest body in the last three days, and 2) the second day's body is less than 30% of the first day's body. Running the evening star test during the 01/03/06 to 05/01/07 period using this modified definition yielded the results shown in Figure 7.11.

We also determined that white space gaps on the third day of the pattern were one of the stronger parameter changes, but significantly reduced the number of trades. Adding that requirement to the modified definition results in the interesting results of Figure 7.12. This is the first set of parameters that shows an annualized ROI above buy and hold with a percentage of winning trades above break even.

FIGURE 7.11:
RESULTS OF MODIFIED EVENING
STAR DURING 01/03/06 TO 05/01/07

EveningStarTester		Winners	Losers	Neutral
Number of trades in test:	1032	505	521	6
Average periods per trade:	5.77	5.82	5.71	5.83
Maximum Profit/Loss:		22.49 %	(29.27)%	
Average Drawdown:	(1.86)%	(0.51)%	(3.19)%	
Average Profit/Loss:	0.06 %	3.02 %	(2.82)%	
Average SPX Profit/Loss:	(0.10)%	0.32 %	(0.51)%	
Probability:		48.93 %	50.48 %	
Average Annual ROI:	3.50 %	189.23 %	(179.99)%	
Annual SPX (Buy & Hold):	14.34 %			
Reward/Risk Ratio:	1.04			
Start test date:	01/03/06			
End test date:	05/01/07			

Interval: Daily
Pricing Summary
Entry price: [Open]
Exit price: [Open]
Exit Summary
Hold for 4 periods

Courtesy of AIQ

The results of Figure 7.12 look interesting. The issue is that only 106 trades were produced during the test period, so the results may not be specific to the test period. The results of testing the modified definition with white space gaps on day three in other test periods is shown in Table 7.3.

Table 7.3 indicates that the modified pattern with day three white space gaps consistently generates 40 to 50 trades a year. It is good that the pattern generates about the same number of trades every year. Systems that generate a bunch of trades in one time period and none in another may be suspect. The problem with this modification to the evening star pattern is since it only generates a few trades every year, it is difficult to add additional filters to investigate further the reasons for these results.

The results of using the pattern beat buy and hold annualized ROI in recent times, and start to fall behind in longer time periods. It may be that the market conditions themselves have a stronger effect on evening star pattern

FIGURE 7.12:
TEST RESULTS OF MODIFIED
EVENING STAR WITH DAY 3 WHITE SPACE GAP

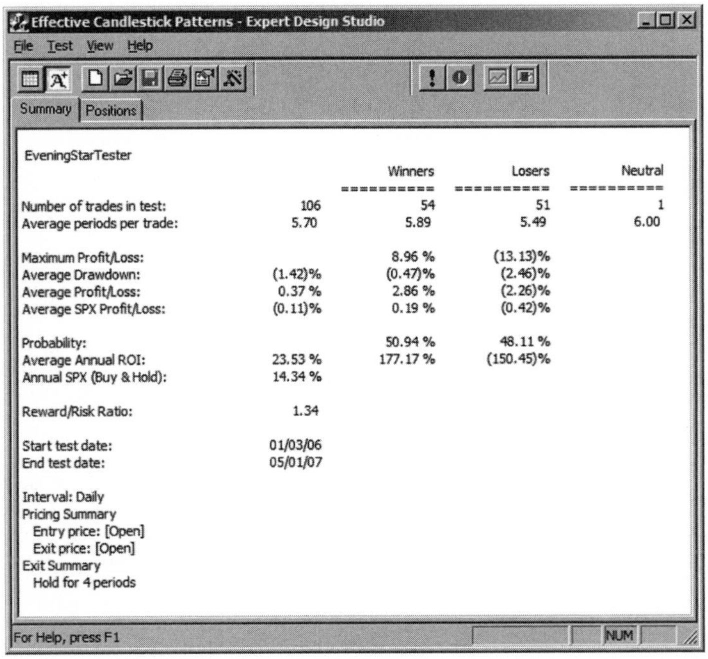

Effective Candlestick Patterns - Expert Design Studio				
File Test View Help				
Summary	Positions			
EveningStarTester		Winners	Losers	Neutral
Number of trades in test:	106	54	51	1
Average periods per trade:	5.70	5.89	5.49	6.00
Maximum Profit/Loss:		8.96 %	(13.13)%	
Average Drawdown:	(1.42)%	(0.47)%	(2.46)%	
Average Profit/Loss:	0.37 %	2.86 %	(2.26)%	
Average SPX Profit/Loss:	(0.11)%	0.19 %	(0.42)%	
Probability:		50.94 %	48.11 %	
Average Annual ROI:	23.53 %	177.17 %	(150.45)%	
Annual SPX (Buy & Hold):	14.34 %			
Reward/Risk Ratio:	1.34			
Start test date:	01/03/06			
End test date:	05/01/07			
Interval: Daily				
Pricing Summary				
Entry price: [Open]				
Exit price: [Open]				
Exit Summary				
Hold for 4 periods				
For Help, press F1			NUM	

Courtesy of AIQ

results than variations in the pattern definition. Since strong bull and bear periods typically last for months not years, it is problematic to test this pattern in a number of bull and bear cycles and still obtain enough trades in each cycle to be significant.

Backtesting has provided us with insights into the pattern, but there are reasonable limits to what can be done. It is similar to a microscope with a given resolution. Looking for things smaller than the resolution of the microscope is problematic. Looking for meaningful results based on fewer and fewer trades can lead to unreliable results. It is not unusual in the process of testing trading patterns to find something in which the results are inconclusive in longer time frames or do not yield enough trades to be statistically significant. When this happens, you simply investigate another path.

TABLE 7.3
MODIFIED PATTERN WITH DAY 3
WHITE SPACE TEST RESULTS IN VARIOUS TIME PERIODS

TEST PERIOD	ANNUALIZED ROI	BUY & HOLD ROI	NUMBER OF TRADES
01/03/06 to 05/01/07	23.53%	14.34%	106
01/03/05 to 05/01/07	16.87%	9.72%	152
01/03/04 to 05/01/07	8.59%	10.09%	205
01/03/03 to 05/01/07	-4.28%	15.90%	266
01/03/02 to 05/01/07	-7.52%	5.52%	304
01/03/97 to 05/01/07	2.81%	9.73%	417

MOD1 EVENING STAR

Removing the third day white space gap requirement and leaving the other changes to the initial pattern definition results in looking for evening stars in uptrending stocks with: a white body on day one of the pattern that is larger than the body size of the previous day; a gap up on the second day of the pattern with a body less than 30% of the first day's body; and a black body on the third day of the pattern that closes in the bottom half of the first day's range. We will refer to this evening star definition as the "mod1" evening star. This definition results in a 3½% annualized ROI during the 01/03/06 to 05/01/07 test period when using a four day holding period, as shown in Figure 7.13.

Since the "white space on day three" parameter change resulted in too few trades, we will now look at other parameter changes and filters for the mod1

FIGURE 7.13:
TEST RESULTS FOR MOD1
EVENING STAR DURING JAN. 2006 TO MAY 2007

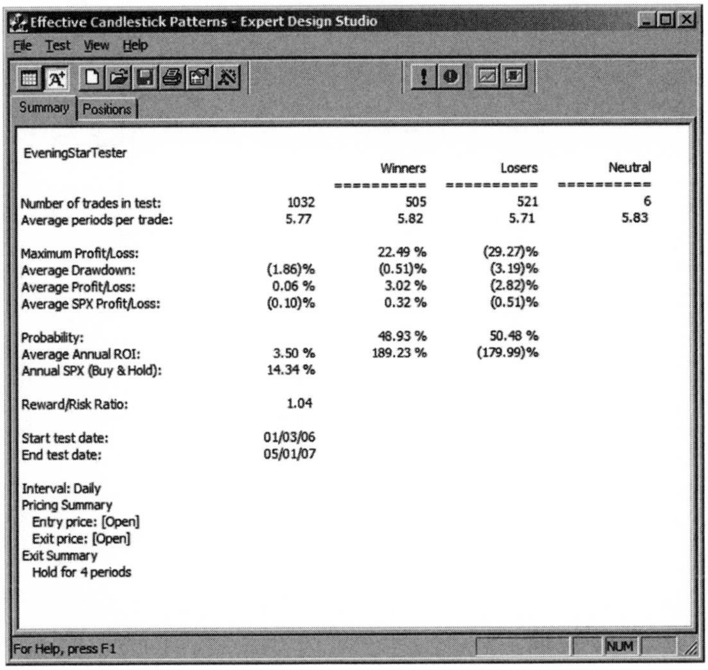

Effective Candlestick Patterns - Expert Design Studio

File Test View Help

Summary | Positions

EveningStarTester

		Winners	Losers	Neutral
Number of trades in test:	1032	505	521	6
Average periods per trade:	5.77	5.82	5.71	5.83
Maximum Profit/Loss:		22.49 %	(29.27)%	
Average Drawdown:	(1.86)%	(0.51)%	(3.19)%	
Average Profit/Loss:	0.06 %	3.02 %	(2.82)%	
Average SPX Profit/Loss:	(0.10)%	0.32 %	(0.51)%	
Probability:		48.93 %	50.48 %	
Average Annual ROI:	3.50 %	189.23 %	(179.99)%	
Annual SPX (Buy & Hold):	14.34 %			
Reward/Risk Ratio:	1.04			
Start test date:	01/03/06			
End test date:	05/01/07			

Interval: Daily
Pricing Summary
Entry price: [Open]
Exit price: [Open]
Exit Summary
Hold for 4 periods

For Help, press F1 NUM

Courtesy of AIQ

evening star to see if we can find a pattern with better results. The mod1 evening star is not a tradable system because it yields an annualized ROI less than buy and hold. We need to find a modification that shows better trading results or use a different pattern for trading.

RECENT HIGH REQUIREMENT

After looking at a number of evening star patterns, it seemed they worked well when the second day of the pattern was the recent high. In these cases, the middle day of the evening star was the peak of the run up, which makes sense since the evening star is a reversal pattern. An example of this type of pattern is shown in Figure 7.14.

One of the issues with trading is it is easy to look at a number of charts and be convinced there is a pattern. The advantage of backtesting is you can look

FIGURE 7.14:
EVENING STAR IS RECENT HIGH IN HSOA ON 05/24/06

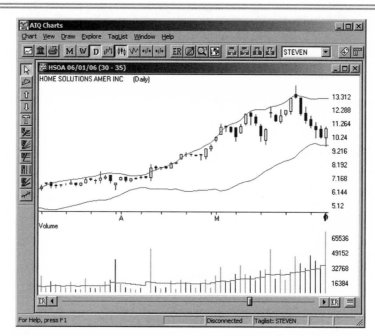

Courtesy of AIQ

at thousands of charts and patterns and determine how often something actually happens. Testing the mod1 evening star with the additional requirement that the pattern occur at a recent high, as shown in Figure 7.14, actually reduced the results slightly and resulted in an annualized ROI under 2% during the 01/03/06 to 05/01/07 test period.

Knowing What Works and What Doesn't

At this point you may be thinking, "Just show me what works." But remember, not all patterns can be made to work; and, it is important to thoroughly understand a pattern before trading it. It is just as important to know which parameters don't maximize results as the ones that do because some days you will see more patterns than you can trade and you will have to prioritize the opportunities. This is where this information becomes vital. The more you understand how a trading pattern works, what affects results and what does not, then the easier it will be to make trades with confidence.

RECENT RUN REQUIREMENT

Another filter that looked promising was to look for evening stars in stocks that were not just in an uptrend, but had shown a strong recent run. The idea is that after a rapid run, many stocks reverse and the evening star would mark the reversal. I looked at all the evening stars using the mod1 definition plus a requirement that the stock had to have run up at least 20% in the last 10 days. An example of this behavior is shown in Figure 7.15.

Taking evening star trades after at least a 20% run up in 10 days sounds like a great idea. It makes sense that after a fast movement a stock would

FIGURE 7.15:
EVENING STAR PATTERN IN
MAMA ON 12/22/06 AFTER RAPID RUN UP

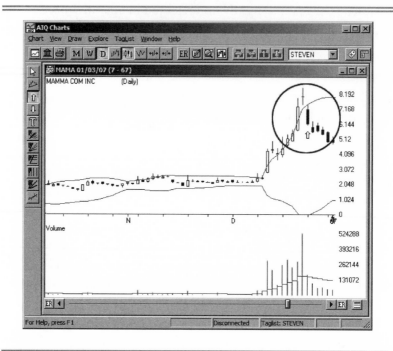

Courtesy of AIQ

retrace. However, traders need to be careful about a few examples and a logical explanation. It is not what sounds good that matters; it's what works. This filter actually reduced results and moved the annualized ROI back into negative territory.

I tried a number of other parameter changes and filters, and most did not turn the evening star pattern into a tradable system. In many cases, the pattern is more susceptible to the market conditions than it is to parameter changes and filters. Because of this discovery, I used a volume filter that helps locate stocks that might be running out of steam.

CREATING MOD2 USING
A VOLUME REQUIREMENT

I added the requirement to the mod1 evening star that the short term average volume be declining and it improved results. The way I calculated the volume decline was to require that the average volume of the five days before the evening star pattern be less than 80% of the average volume of the last 25 days. An example of this declining volume pattern is shown in Figure 7.16, in which the low volume days preceding the formation of the evening star pattern are marked by down arrows in the volume portion of the chart.

Test results for declining volume patterns with the mod1 evening star resulted in promising results as shown in Figure 7.17. During the 01/03/06 to 05/01/07 test period, this new filter resulted in the most interesting results

FIGURE 7.16:
DECLINING AVERAGE VOLUME
EVENING STAR IN ARD ON 02/27/07

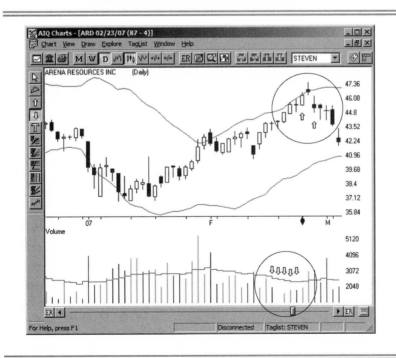

Courtesy of AIQ

```
Effective Candlestick Patterns - Expert Design Studio                    _ □ X
File  Test  View  Help

  □ A  □ ☞ 🖫 🖨 🗗 🗚              ! ●  🖾 🔲

Summary │ Positions │

  EveningStarTester
                                        Winners      Losers      Neutral
                                     ===========  ===========  ===========
  Number of trades in test:      243       131          111            1
  Average periods per trade:     5.71      5.88         5.51         6.00

  Maximum Profit/Loss:                     12.20 %      (10.95)%
  Average Drawdown:           (1.60)%      (0.50)%      (2.92)%
  Average Profit/Loss:          0.43 %      2.93 %      (2.53)%
  Average SPX Profit/Loss:      0.04 %      0.46 %      (0.46)%

  Probability:                             53.91 %      45.68 %
  Average Annual ROI:          27.24 %    182.01 %     (167.20)%
  Annual SPX (Buy & Hold):     14.34 %

  Reward/Risk Ratio:            1.37

  Start test date:           01/03/06
  End test date:             05/01/07

  Interval: Daily
  Pricing Summary
    Entry price: [Open]
    Exit price: [Open]
  Exit Summary
    Hold for 4 periods

For Help, press F1                                        NUM
```

Courtesy of AIQ

seen so far. The 27% annualized ROI is about double buy and hold and the pattern shows winning trades more than 53% of the time while producing a respectable 243 trades. Amazing how one simple filter can make quite a difference; the issue of course is whether we also see positive results in other time frames.

Testing the mod1 evening star with declining volume, which we will now call the mod2 evening star, in six different time periods yielded the results shown in Table 7.4. The mod2 pattern only showed a loss in one period, a period that included the worst NASDAQ bear market in history. In the other five time periods, the results beat buy and hold by 2-to-1 in four of the periods and were about the same in the other. This represents a significant improvement over the results of Table 7.3, while at the same time producing more trades.

These results are the beginning of an interesting trading pattern that may be useful in the trader's toolbox. I would not trade the basic evening star as first defined, since the results were less than buy and hold and showed losing trades most of the time. Adding the parameter changes and filters discussed above turned the original pattern from something I would pass on into something worth considering.

TABLE 7.4
MOD2 PATTERN TEST RESULTS IN DIFFERENT TIME PERIODS

TEST PERIOD	ANNUALIZED ROI	BUY & HOLD ROI	NUMBER OF TRADES
01/03/06 to 05/01/07	27.24%	14.34%	243
01/03/05 to 05/01/07	29.64%	9.72%	362
01/03/04 to 05/01/07	26.83%	10.09%	488
01/03/03 to 05/01/07	15.25%	15.90%	646
01/03/02 to 05/01/07	12.37%	5.52%	720
01/03/97 to 05/01/07	-2.96%	9.73%	1,035

EVENING STAR PATTERN SUMMARY

After all of our backtesting, the test results presented here indicate that the results of trading the evening star pattern may be improved by requiring that the third day of the pattern has a body length that is the largest body length in the last five days. Trading results can also be improved by: using patterns that show white space gaps on the third day; trading patterns where the second day has a white, not a black, body; using patterns whose first day's body is the largest body in the last three trading days; andlooking for patterns whose recent average volume is declining.

The testing also indicates that results are not improved, or may be diminished, when using the evening star pattern in the following conditions: when the third day of the three day pattern opens with a gap down; using patterns that show white space gaps on the second day of the pattern; using patterns that occur at a recent high; and picking patterns that show rapid runs with a price movement of at least twenty percent in ten days.

The improved evening star pattern requirements are:
• The stock must be in an uptrend.
• The simple average of the volume during the five days before the evening star must be less than the average volume of the past 25 days.
• Day one requires:
    ~ A white body.
    ~ A body larger than the previous day's body.
• Day two requires:
    ~ Either color body.
    ~ A body less than 30% of the previous day's body.
    ~ A gap up, defined as the opening being above the previous day's close.
• Day three requires:
    ~ A black body.
    ~ A close below the midpoint of the range of day one.

Remember, backtesting does not guarantee any future result. It is unlikely to find a realistic pattern that works all the time. Trading is a statistical business where traders must understand how often their pattern may be expected to win and lose, and they must adjust their strategies accordingly. Trading will always present risks, and good traders must learn how to manage those risks through careful analysis of the market conditions and adjustments to exit strategies, number of trading positions, and position sizes.

─|CHAPTER 8|─

MARKET ADAPTIVE
TRADING TECHNIQUES

In the previous chapters of this book, we looked at several common candlestick patterns and used backtesting techniques to determine how often they were successful. We also developed an understanding of how variations of the pattern definition, and different filters, affect trading results. Developing, testing, and understanding a set of tools, or trading patterns, is one of the key steps in successful trading.

Another key requirement of successful trading is the ability to analyze the current market conditions in order to determine appropriate risk levels and to select the best patterns for trading. Remember, most patterns are more effective in certain market conditions and matching the right tool to the job can help us trade more effectively. Trading the same pattern all the time may just churn the account. Traders need to use their research to trade the most statistically favorable patterns.

Analyzing the price and volume patterns in the market and then selecting the best trading tools and using appropriate risk management is a process I refer to as market adaptive trading (MAT). Since the market will not adapt to us, we must adapt to it. Trying to predict what the market will do, or to what level it will move, is difficult to do and, more importantly, not necessary. Successful traders analyze the current market conditions and then develop a trading plan that outlines what the market would have to do to make them focus on longs, shorts, or cash; in addition, they determine how much risk to take in a given market environment.

The market has three basic modes; it can be trending up, trending down, or moving within a trading range. As shown by our candlestick pattern testing, most trading tools work best in a trending environment; and thus, when the market is trending, I tend to trade more positions and use larger position sizes. Trading ranges diminish the results of many trading patterns, and I compensate for the increased risk by reducing position sizes and the number of positions I trade.

Trend lines are one of the best tools for determining when the market is moving from one mode to another. If the market is in an uptrend, then it has to break an ascending trend line to move to a significant basing area or start a downtrend. Similarly if the market is in a downtrend, it has to break a descending trend line in order to form a significant base or start a new uptrend. Trend line breaks are usually a time to adjust risk by changing position sizes and the number of positions being traded.

Trend lines drawn on the NASDAQ chart are one of the trader's best friends. When the NASDAQ is trading above an ascending trend line, I focus on trading longs using patterns that have tested well in bullish markets. When the market is moving below a descending trend line, I focus on trading patterns that have tested well in bearish environments. When the market breaks a trend line, it is a call to action. It indicates that conditions may be changing, and I reduce risk by reducing position sizes until the market makes its intentions clear.

The Market Doesn't Care What You Believe

Market adaptive trading is not developing a trading plan based on what you feel the market will do, or based on what the "experts" are saying it will do. In short, no one knows what the market will do; it is best to make a plan for each of the three basic actions that market can take, then trade the plan.

Listen to the market, not what people are saying about it. For example, at a recent trading conference I heard the following statements from those who are considered market experts.

- I continue to believe oil stocks are going to pull back.

- I didn't make money in it the last time I got involved and am inclined to believe that the best way to handle an investment or trade in BAX is employing patience.

- I believe that this instrument will deliver gains from this point going forward. That is why I am involved. No other reason.

The issue with all these statements is that they are presenting a belief, with no real information about why it might be true. It is great that someone believes oil stocks will pull back, or that some stock will deliver gains going foreword. The fundamental issue, of course, is that the market does not care what we believe. We can believe something as strongly as we want, the market will not care.

The market shows us what it thinks through price and volume patterns. Learning to read these patterns is a key part of trading success. Predicting how far the market is going to move, or what the year end closing value will be has little value since no one has been able to consistently do this year after year. However, reading the market's price and volume patterns to determine how much risk to be taking and what tools to be using is something that can be of great benefit to traders.

Rather than trying to forecast direction, traders should focus on identifying key trigger levels and then trading with the market. Traders need to use tools from their trading tool box that are appropriate for the current market conditions. Knowing how each of the tools in the trading tool box performs in each of the basic market modes allows traders to select the most appropriate tool to be using. Using the same trading tool in all market conditions will just give traders a lot of practice exercising stops.

There are several steps to developing a market adaptive trading (MAT) plan.

Step One: Develop, test, and understand several trading patterns. These are the tools in the trader's tool box. The first seven chapters of this book have outlined this process for several candlestick patterns.

Step Two: Understand basic market statistics. If traders do not know how the market reacts in common situations like new highs, new lows, gaps, closing in the top or bottom of the range, etc., then they cannot capitalize on the fact that these common situations can provide leverage for knowledgeable traders.

Step Three: Use trend lines on the NASDAQ chart. This technique keeps traders focused on using the right tools for the job and helps them determine when to reduce risks.

Step Four: Write down your daily trading plan. Look at the current market conditions and determine if they are favorable to trading longs, shorts, or remaining in cash. If the market is in a clear trend, then normal position sizes may be used. If the market is in a trading range, then half size positions may help compensate for the increased risk.

Now, let's look at each of these steps in more detail.

MAT STEP ONE: DEVELOP, TEST, AND UNDERSTAND TRADING TOOLS

The first step in market adaptive trading is to develop, test, and understand several trading patterns. These are the tools in the trader's tool box. As we have seen, testing identifies filters that can improve a pattern's trading results and the best market conditions in which to use the pattern. We can then use trend lines to determine when to switch between different trading tools.

The trading tools we have developed so far are the bullish engulfing, bearish engulfing, hammer, hanging man, morning star, and evening star candlestick patterns. These are the tools available to us for trading and should be selected for use when the market conditions are most favorable for a particular pattern. A quick summary of what we've learned is below.

BULLISH ENGULFING PATTERN SUMMARY

The bullish engulfing pattern is one that shows positive results in multiple timeframes. We saw that two simple additions to the basic pattern definition significantly improved the results. This trading pattern should be avoided when the market is in a downtrend.

The pattern was also significantly improved by focusing on trading those that have above average volume on the first day. The effort put into backtesting allowed us to quickly analyze the results of thousands of trades and find two simple techniques to nearly triple the annualized ROI for this pattern.

BEARISH ENGULFING PATTERN SUMMARY

We found that the bearish engulfing pattern may be improved by: using it in downtrending or bearish markets; using a three to five day holding period; using it on higher-priced stocks; looking for volume on the second day of the pattern that is larger that the volume on the first day of the pattern; and taking patterns when the top of the second day's body is at least 15% of the day's range above the top of the first day's body.

Based on the test results shown in chapter three I would not trade the basic bearish engulfing pattern in all markets. I would confine its use to bear market conditions, and I would use the volume filter. It would not be the only pattern I trade, but is an interesting addition to the trader's tool box and one of the patterns I look at when the conditions are right.

HAMMER PATTERN SUMMARY

Through our testing, we found that the hammer pattern may be improved by: requiring the upper shadow be at least 5% of the day's range; trading stocks priced under $30, trading stocks with average daily volume under a million shares; trading with volume at 160% or more of the previous day's volume; trading hammers whose range is the largest range of the last 5 days.

The results in chapter four indicate that the basic hammer pattern can be significantly improved by only trading the pattern when the day's trading range is the largest of the last five sessions. Since the wide range hammer filter nearly doubles annualized ROI in tests involving two different timeframes and covering almost five years, it is something worth considering when trading this pattern. The wide range hammer generally does not test well during periods when the market is in a downtrend.

HANGING MAN PATTERN SUMMARY

Our results showed that the hanging man pattern may be improved by trading the pattern in bearish markets and requiring the pattern to occur as the highest high of the last five days. Even with these improvements, the hanging man pattern was not as effective as the others. Some patterns are good tools to use, and some patterns are best left alone.

The basic hanging man trading pattern, discussed in chapter five, does not produce favorable results when used continuously through a variety of market conditions. It is not an all-weather tool. It does show good results in several downtrending or bear markets. In fact, the market conditions have a much stronger effect on these results than any of the other filters tested. It should be avoided in uptrending or bullish markets. A holding time around five days seems to work best, and patterns that occur around recent highs may be more productive.

MORNING STAR PATTERN SUMMARY

Our test results indicate that the results of the morning star pattern may be improved by: trading patterns with a first day's black body larger than the previous day's body; requiring the second day's body to be less than 60% of the day's range; requiring the close of the second day of the pattern to be below the low of the first day of the pattern, when the second day of the pattern has a black body; and using a four to five day holding period.

In chapter six we found that the basic morning star pattern is statistically equal to a coin flip and after testing a number of different modifications and variations to the basic morning star definition, we found that slight changes to the definition of the morning star can significantly improve results. These slight changes to the definition take the pattern from a break even result to something that beats buy and hold and shows about 59% of the trades as profitable.

EVENING STAR PATTERN SUMMARY

After our testing, we found that the evening star pattern may be improved by: requiring that the third day of the pattern has a body length that is the largest body length in the last five days; taking evening star patterns with white space gaps on the third day; having the body on the second day of the pattern be white; and requiring the first day's body to be the largest in the last three days, when recent average volume is declining.

The test results for the evening star pattern shown in chapter seven showed why I would not trade the basic evening star as first defined since the results were less than buy and hold and it showed losing trades most of the time. Using backtesting to analyze various parameter changes and filters resulted in changes that turned the original pattern from something I would pass on to something I would consider using.

Now that we have a better understanding of how each of the candlestick patterns perform, and have identified specific ways to improve the results of each pattern, we need to look at some basic market statistics. Knowing what the market typically does in common situations helps us to determine whether or not to be taking trades, and if so, how aggressively to be trading. There is a lot more to successful trading than just identifying a pattern and entering a trade.

MAT STEP TWO:
UNDERSTANDING BASIC MARKET STATISTICS

The second step in developing a market adaptive trading plan is to understand basic market statistics. If traders do not know how the market reacts in common situations like new highs, new lows, gaps, closing in the top or bottom of the range, etc., then they cannot capitalize on the fact that these common situations can provide leverage for knowledgeable traders. Understanding how the market usually behaves in these common situations helps traders adjust their position sizes and the number of positions being traded to more closely match the risk levels in the market.

The market rarely goes straight up or down; it usually runs a bit, then pulls back, then runs some more. Should traders be more aggressive on taking trades after the market has run up a bit, or should they wait and be more aggressive after the market has pulled back? Knowing how the market usually behaves after run ups or pullbacks allows traders to better position themselves to profit when the market does the statistically "normal" thing.

Understanding how the market usually behaves in a given situation allows traders to adjust their trading style and risk management to the current market conditions. For example, if it is better to buy new lows than new highs, then traders could take larger positions and more of them when the market is making new lows and take more profits when the market is making new highs. The information below shares research into how the market typically reacts to common situations so traders can position appropriately.

SHOULD YOU BUY AT NEW HIGHS OR NEW LOWS?

The idea of trading is to be positioned to profit if the market does the normal or usual thing in a given situation, and this is where basic market statistics come into play.

For example, let's look at the question: are you better off buying when the market is making new highs or new lows? Most traders have an opinion on this, but very few have actually tested the proposition to determine what the best answer is. Remember, don't rely on opinions—trading based on testing and analysis is what gives you an edge.

Figure 8.1 shows the test results for testing the idea of buying when the market makes a new high. The test covered a four-year period during which the market was purchased whenever it made a 10 day high. The position was

FIGURE 8.1:
BUYING 10 DAY HIGHS

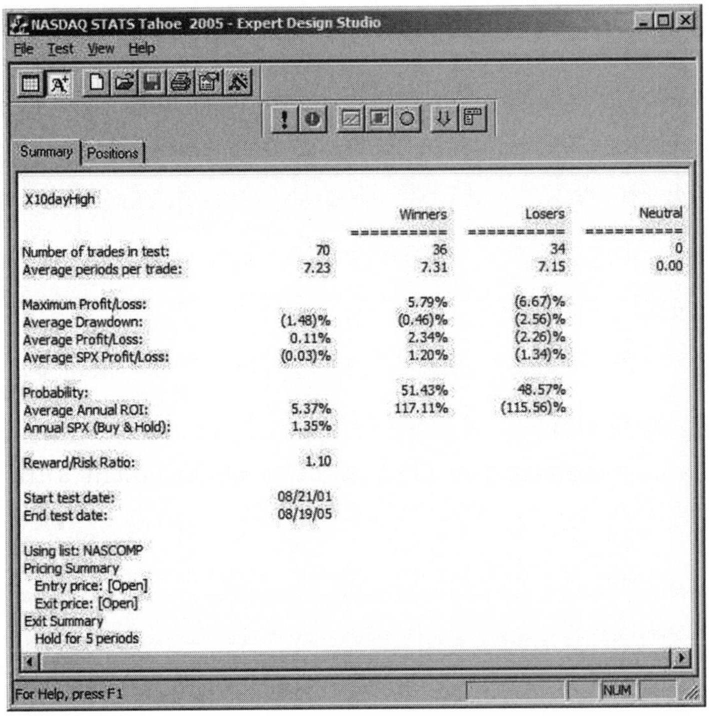

X10dayHigh		Winners	Losers	Neutral
Number of trades in test:	70	36	34	0
Average periods per trade:	7.23	7.31	7.15	0.00
Maximum Profit/Loss:		5.79%	(6.67)%	
Average Drawdown:	(1.48)%	(0.46)%	(2.56)%	
Average Profit/Loss:	0.11%	2.34%	(2.26)%	
Average SPX Profit/Loss:	(0.03)%	1.20%	(1.34)%	
Probability:		51.43%	48.57%	
Average Annual ROI:	5.37%	117.11%	(115.56)%	
Annual SPX (Buy & Hold):	1.35%			
Reward/Risk Ratio:	1.10			
Start test date:	08/21/01			
End test date:	08/19/05			

Using list: NASCOMP
Pricing Summary
Entry price: [Open]
Exit price: [Open]
Exit Summary
Hold for 5 periods

Courtesy of AIQ

held for five days and then closed. The results indicate winning positions slightly over half the time and an annualized ROI of more than 5%.

What if instead of buying the market when it is making a new 10 day high, we buy the market when it is making a new 10 day low? The results are very interesting. As shown in Figure 8.2, buying new 10 day lows resulted in about the same percentage of winning trades as buying 10 day highs. The difference was that buying 10 day lows results tripled the annualized ROI. This is a significant difference and worth further investigation.

In order to check whether or not there is something unusual about 10 day highs and lows, I repeated the experiment using 20 day highs and lows. Figure 8.3 shows the four test results for buying the market when it makes a 20 day high, holding for five days, then closing the position. This technique

FIGURE 8.2:
BUYING 10 DAY LOWS

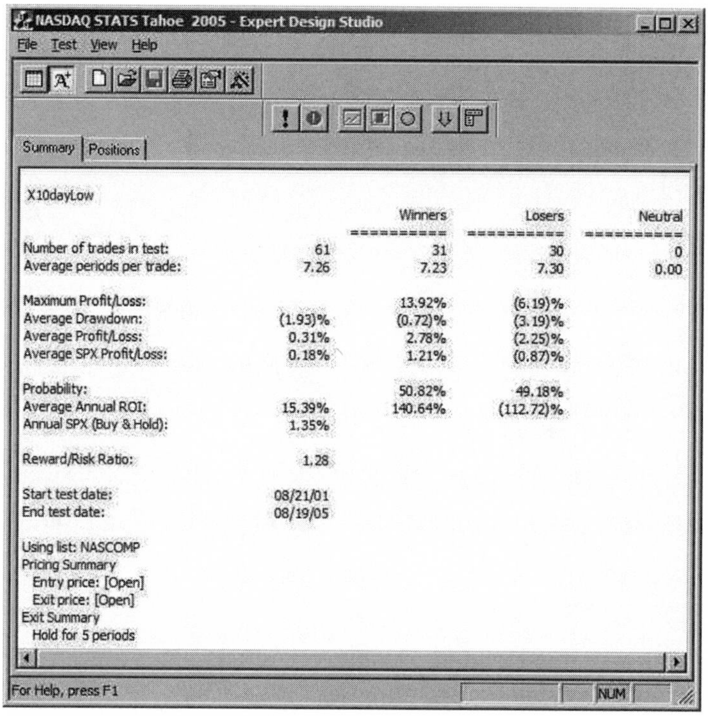
NASDAQ STATS Tahoe 2005 - Expert Design Studio

File Test View Help

Summary | Positions

X10dayLow

		Winners	Losers	Neutral
		==========	==========	==========
Number of trades in test:	61	31	30	0
Average periods per trade:	7.26	7.23	7.30	0.00
Maximum Profit/Loss:		13.92%	(6.19)%	
Average Drawdown:	(1.93)%	(0.72)%	(3.19)%	
Average Profit/Loss:	0.31%	2.78%	(2.25)%	
Average SPX Profit/Loss:	0.18%	1.21%	(0.87)%	
Probability:		50.82%	49.18%	
Average Annual ROI:	15.39%	140.64%	(112.72)%	
Annual SPX (Buy & Hold):	1.35%			
Reward/Risk Ratio:	1.28			
Start test date:	08/21/01			
End test date:	08/19/05			

Using list: NASCOMP
Pricing Summary
Entry price: [Open]
Exit price: [Open]
Exit Summary
Hold for 5 periods

For Help, press F1 NUM

Courtesy of AIQ

FIGURE 8.3:
BUYING 20 DAY HIGHS

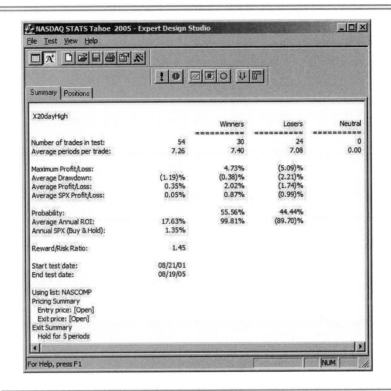

Courtesy of AIQ

showed significantly better results than buying 10 day highs, and slightly better results than buying 10 day lows.

Figure 8.4 shows the four test results for buying the market when it makes a 20 day low. The results show an annualized ROI about double that for buying 20 day highs. Whether considering 10 or 20 day periods, the four year test results indicate that buying when the market is making new lows yields at least twice the annualized ROI than obtained by buying when the market is making new highs.

Buying extended markets can be profitable. Buying market pullbacks can be more profitable. This is one reason why there are so many different pullback trading systems. I have developed and tested several different ones that I use every day. Would I just blindly buy the market every time it pulls back? No,

Courtesy of AIQ

there is, of course, more to the story; however, when the market has pulled back on light volume after running up on strong volume, I start trading larger positions and more of them. I adapt my trading style to the rhythm of the market based on the test results.

The test results for buying at new highs and new lows indicate that buying after the market has pulled back yields better results than buying after the market has run up. Given this data, I adapt to what the market is doing by increasing my market exposure when it bounces after a pullback. I do not trade the same number of positions or use the same position sizes all the time. I adjust my position sizes and number of trading positions based on the risk level that the market is presenting.

HOW SHOULD YOU RESPOND TO GAPS?

Traders frequently ask how to respond to times when the market gaps. Once again, the way to develop a plan is to use backtesting techniques to see what happens when the market gaps at the open. In the 100 days prior to 8/19/05, the NASDAQ gapped up 50 times and filled the gap up 64% of the time. It gapped down 50 times and filled the gap down 76% of the time. During this period, opening gaps were common and quite likely to be filled before the end of the day.

I tested gaps in two additional 100 day periods to see if the pattern held. In the 100 days prior to 5/19/05, the NASDAQ gapped up 59 times and filled the gap up 69% of the time. It gapped down 41 times and filled the gap down 78% of the time. In the 100 days prior to 2/18/05, the NASDAQ gapped up 52 times and filled the gap up 63% of the time. It gapped down 48 times and filled the gap down 83% of the time. Once again, the data indicates that opening gaps are common and that they are usually filled on the day they occur.

Based on this data and a number of years of observing the market, I respond to the market's tendency to gap at the open by typically not trading during the first 20 to 30 minutes of trading. This gives the market a chance to settle down and pick a direction after the opening gap. The market often moves in the direction of the gap after filling it, so waiting a bit may provide the opportunity for a slightly better price. Once again we can use the results of testing the market to add to our collection of ways to adapt our trading to the market's tendencies.

HOW SHOULD YOU RESPOND TO TOP OF THE RANGE CLOSES?

I once heard a speaker say that since the market had closed near the top of its range, it would be moving up tomorrow. Once again, I would advise you to test ideas and see if they really provide an edge in trading. This is what market adaptive trading is all about—gathering data on how the market typically behaves in common situations, then using that data to determine how aggressive to trade. I ran several tests to look at whether or not the market closed up the day after closing in the top 10% of its range and found the following:

- In the 100 days prior to 8/19/05, the market closed in the top 10% of the range 29 times and was up the next day 12 times.
- In the 100 days prior to 5/19/05, the market closed in the top 10% of the range 20 times and was up the next day 6 times.
- In the 100 days prior to 2/18/05, the market closed in the top 10% of the range 23 times and was up the next day 13 times.

Based on this data it appears that closing in the top part of the day's trading range does not strongly influence the direction that the market takes the next day. It would not be wise to increase the number of trading positions being traded or the position sizes based on the market closing in the top part of the daily range.

When the test data indicates there is an edge, like buying into pullbacks, I increase my position sizes because the odds favor positive results. This does not imply that it always works, just that over the long run the odds are favorable. When I find information like the data above indicating that closes in the top part of the range do not strongly affect the next day's direction, then I do not increase position sizes when that occurs because there is no advantage or edge to it. Market adaptive trading is about finding conditions that give you an edge an then using that to your advantage.

SHOULD YOU TIME THE MARKET USING INDICATORS?

Some traders monitor the stochastic or MACD indicators to help them determine whether or not to be in the market. Most indicators by themselves do not test well in terms of timing the market. Figure 8.5 shows the results of testing the stochastic indicator for market timing. A simple test involved buying the market when the stochastic moved from under 20 to above 20, holding the position for five days, and then closing it. During the three year test period, this technique produced winning trades less than half the time. I am not interested in using something that is right less than half the time to determine when to be in or out of the market.

MARKET TIMING WITH THE STOCHASTIC INDICATOR

Courtesy of AIQ

Figure 8.6 shows the results of a three year test using the stochastic indicator to time shorts. The market was shorted when the stochastic fell from above 80 to below 80. Positions were held for five days and then closed. During this test period, less than half of the short trades were profitable.

I have learned to focus on the price and volume patterns of the market and do not rely on indicators. I have found that using trend lines on the NASDAQ is more productive than the indicators I've tested. The trick to using trend lines and support/resistance levels is to know what to do when the market approaches or breaks them.

TIMING SHORTS WITH THE STOCHASTIC INDICATOR

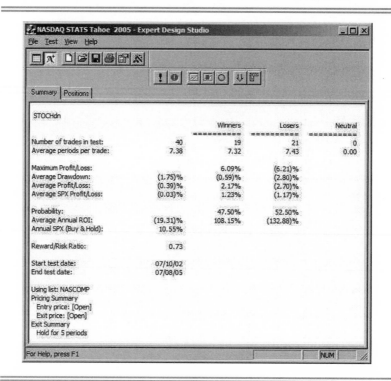

Courtesy of AIQ

MARKET BEHAVIOR CHECKLIST

Based on these tests and a number of others, I have formed a basic check list to consider when trading. These are not hard and fast rules, but are a part of the things I take into consideration when reviewing whether or not to take a trade and how much to risk.

- Trade 10 or 20 day lows more aggressively than breakouts to new highs.
- The market gaps at the open a vast majority of the time; gaps are filled 2/3 of the time. Keep your powder dry on the open.
- Closing in the top of the range does not imply the market will be up the next day.

- The market is up more than four days in a row infrequently, so be cautious buying into runs.

- The market rarely trades less than 10 points or more than 35 points in a day. Be careful entering after a big move. If the market has not moved 10 points, watch for an entry.

There is a lot more market data that can be useful in determining when to trade and when to stand aside. An entire book could easily be devoted to the subject. The point here is that knowing how the market usually behaves can guide trading actions. For example since buying market lows shows better test results than buying market highs, I tend to increase position sizes when the market is bouncing from a low volume pullback.

MAT STEP THREE: USING TREND LINES

The third step in market adaptive trading is using trend lines on the NASDAQ chart to determine which tool to use and when to reduce risk. Trading patterns such as the bullish engulfing and hammer patterns that have shown good testing results in bull markets should be considered when the market is trading above an ascending trend line. Trading patterns that have shown good test results when the market is bearish, such as the hanging man and the bearish engulfing patterns, should be considered when the market is trading below a descending trend line.

Selecting tools from the trader's tool box based on whether the market is trading above an ascending or below a descending trend line can keep traders using the best available tools as the market cycles between its three basic modes. There is no guesswork or emotion involved in the process. The third step of market adaptive trading simply matches well-tested tools to the current market environment using trend lines.

TREND LINE BREAKS ARE A CALL TO ACTION

Figure 8.7 shows an eight-month period in which the market showed bullish and bearish periods, yet it ended up at about the same level that it was when

FIGURE 8.7:
MARKET TRADING RANGE

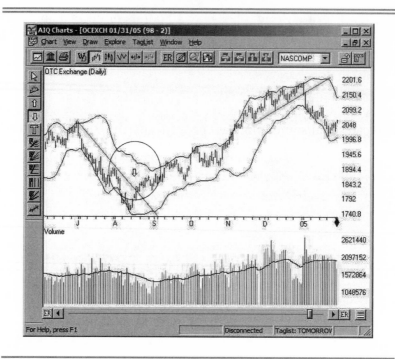

Courtesy of AIQ

the period started. Many buy and hold investors would be at about the same place where they started the eight-month period. Short term traders had significant opportunities to profit from both the bullish and bearish environments by using trend lines for guidance.

As shown in Figure 8.7 bullish and bearish periods in the market tend to end with trend line breaks. When the market was trading beneath the descending trend line during July and August, traders should have focused on trading short setups and avoiding longs. The research in the previous chapters has identified patterns that perform better in bearish environments and also patterns that should not be used in bearish environments.

At some point all trend lines are broken. During the market period shown in Figure 8.7, the bearish period, marked by the descending trend line, ended in the middle of August with a trend line break (marked by the down arrow).

The bullish period also ended with the break of an ascending trend line in late December.

A trend line break is not necessarily the end of the current trend, but it is a call to action. When a descending trend line is broken, the market may begin a new uptrend, or it may base for awhile before picking a new direction, or in some cases it may be a false breakout and the original trend may continue. One of the keys to market adaptive trading is to realize that a trend line break indicates that something has changed, and the trader must react to it.

After a trend line break, there is a period of uncertainty while the market picks its next direction. Uncertainty in trading implies increased risk. Traders should compensate for increased risk by reducing position sizes and also the number of positions being traded. Once the market makes its next direction clear, traders can return to the original position sizes and number of positions traded.

The break of a descending trend line indicates that a change *may* occur, not that a change will occur. After the break of a descending trend line, a new uptrend is not confirmed until the market shows confirmation by making a higher low and then a higher high. At this point a new ascending trend line may be drawn since an uptrend is by definition a series of higher highs and higher lows. Again, traders should maintain a lower risk profile until the market confirms its new uptrend.

Figure 8.8 shows a close-up view of the market's action after the break of the descending trend line shown in Figure 8.7. After the initial trend line break (noted by the down arrow), traders should reduce risks and look for confirmation of the market's next move. The market moved up for seven sessions after the break of the descending trend line, pulled back for two sessions, and then moved up for seven sessions. After this three week period, the market had formed a higher low and a higher high as noted by the up arrows.

Once the market has made a higher low and a higher high, it is by definition in an uptrend. At this point traders may become more aggressive and trade patterns that have tested well in bullish environments. Traders should then draw a new ascending trend line using the lowest low under the original

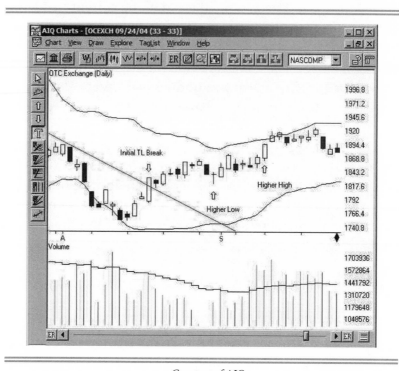

Courtesy of AIQ

descending trend line and the new higher low, and trade bullish patterns until the ascending trend line is broken.

The reason for reducing risks after the break of the descending trend line is that the market does not always go directly to a bullish environment after the break of a descending trend line. It may move up a few days and then continue down, or it may move sideways for a bit and then continue down. Figure 8.9 shows a time when the market broke above a descending trend line for a few days and then continued down. In this case trading at reduced risk levels on the long side after the break of the descending trend line would have been a good way to minimize losses and protect previous profits.

Reducing position sizes and the number of positions traded during this period would help to preserve profits. Also, if the market moves sideways

FIGURE 8.9:
NOT ALL DESCENDING TREND
LINE BREAKS ARE THE START OF A NEW BULLISH PHASE

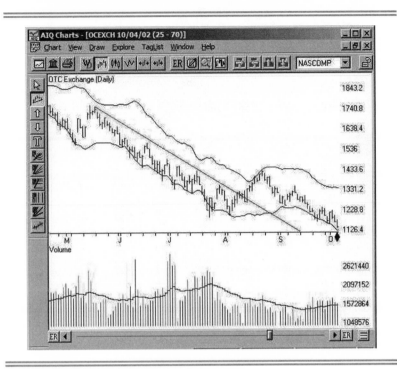

Courtesy of AIQ

for a bit, the environment is often not friendly to traders. Waiting for confirmation reduces the money at risk while the market is makes up its mind on what it wants to do next.

Figure 8.10 shows the break of an ascending trend line. Traders should be focused on trading long patterns that have been shown to be effective in bullish markets while the market is above the ascending trend line. When the trend line break occurs, it indicates that the market conditions may be changing. Because of the trend line break, there is more uncertainty in regards to which direction the market will move next. Traders should respond to uncertainty by reducing risk.

After the break of the ascending trend line, traders should begin to look for signs that would confirm a new trend. If the market makes a lower low, and

FIGURE 8.10:
ASCENDING TREND LINE BREAK

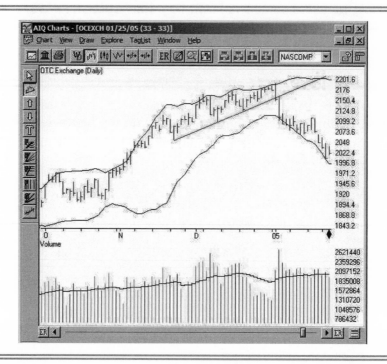

Courtesy of AIQ

a lower high, then by definition it is downtrending; and, traders should draw a new descending trend line from the recent high above the ascending trend line to the new higher high that forms below it. Once the market confirms a new downtrend, traders should focus on trading shorts using patterns that have tested well in bearish environments.

If instead of establishing a new downtrend the market just drops for a bit and then continues up, traders should draw a new ascending trend line using the new low formed once the market makes a higher high and confirms that it is back in an uptrend. One of the tricks to trading is not to care which way the market goes, or to get all caught up in trying to predict direction. It is important to just observe the market and adjust your risk levels to what it does.

DEALING WITH TRADING RANGE ENVIRONMENTS

The market is not always in a clear up or down trend, sometimes it is range bound and just moves back and for the between two levels for awhile. An example of this type of trading range market is shown in Figure 8.11. There are two types of trading ranges, and the trader must respond differently to each one.

A narrow trading range, when the market moves between support and resistance in less than four days, should be avoided. Narrow trading ranges do not provide enough time for swing trades to work. The good news is that they do not happen often and are usually followed by strong moves that provide much better trading opportunities.

FIGURE 8.11:
TRADING RANGE MARKET

Courtesy of AIQ

Wide trading ranges, where it takes the market more than four days to move between support and resistance can be traded by switching between long and short patterns using the following procedure:

- When the market bounces off the bottom of the range, take long trades.
- Close long trades when the market approaches the top of the range.
- When the market retraces from the top of the range, take short trades.
- Close shorts when the market approaches the bottom of the range.

In trading range environments, I try to pick off the initial pop when a setup triggers. This is not an environment where you want to "give them room to run." I usually need a good reason to hold for more than three days. For example, if the market and my stock are moving up on increasing volume, I would hold longer.

The reason for taking quick profits in trading range markets is that almost by definition most stocks cannot run very far when the market is in a trading range. The market is the sum of a large number of stocks. If most of them were triggering and running for awhile, then the market would sum all these runs and have to be trending up. Trading ranges exist because most stocks run for a few days and then pull back, and a lot of stocks doing this results in the market moving up and then retracing. Because most stocks tend to "pop and drop" when the market is in a trading range, I want to use short holding times to just pick off a series of "pops" in different stocks. This means I'm piecing together a trend in my account while the market is oscillating back and forth.

MAT STEP FOUR: WRITING YOUR DAILY TRADING PLAN

The fourth step in market adaptive trading is writing down your daily trading plan. The process is to look at the current market conditions and determine if they are favorable to trading longs, shorts, or remaining in cash. If the market is in a clear trend, then normal position sizes may be used. If the market is in a trading range, then half size positions may help compensate for the increased risk that the market typically presents in trading ranges.

Using smaller position sizes when the market transitions from a trend to a trading range will also help protect the profits made during the more favorable trending period. Many trading patterns show a higher percentage of winners during market trends than they do when the market is in a trading range. If you reduce your position sizes while the market is in a trading range, you are adapting to the market by compensating for periods of increased risk caused by lower winning percentages.

These techniques are fairly simple, but it takes a lot of practice to get good at them. Nothing in trading is a magic bullet. It takes time, effort, and money (e.g., some losses) to learn trading techniques. One of the best ways I have found to improve results is to write down my market analysis and trading plan every evening. In this I include an analysis of the key market levels and volume patterns as well as what would make me take longs, take shorts, or remain in cash.

The process of writing out my trading strategy and market analysis grew into publishing *The Timely Trades Letter*. Whether or not you decide to use a newsletter, or work alone, it is important to write out your market analysis and trading strategy. There is something about writing it down that makes you really think it through. Trading on emotion or gut feel is usually a bad idea. Having a well thought out plan helps keep you focused on what is important.

The best way to illustrate the fourth step in MAT is by a couple of examples. On the following pages, we show two examples of trading plans to help illustrate the points made above. Refer to the market charts associated with each example in order to see what the current market conditions were at the time the trading plans were written.

EXAMPLE TRADING PLAN: TREND LINE BREAK TO TRADING RANGE

Figure 8.12 shows the market as of December 10, 2006. The trading plan as published in *The Timely Trades Letter* is reprinted on the next page. Note that trend lines are used to provide trading guidance along with what the market's volume pattern is implying about risk levels. This same type of analysis is the part of market adaptive trading that serves as a guide to the next day's trading. Also note that the trading plan outlines when to take longs, when to take shorts, and how the number of trading positions should be adjusted based on what the market is doing. Analyzing the market and knowing what will cause me to go long, go short, or increase/reduce the number of trading positions helps take the emotion out of trading and allows me to focus on what the market is actually doing before I react to it.

FIGURE 8.12:
DECEMBER 2006 MARKET CONDITIONS

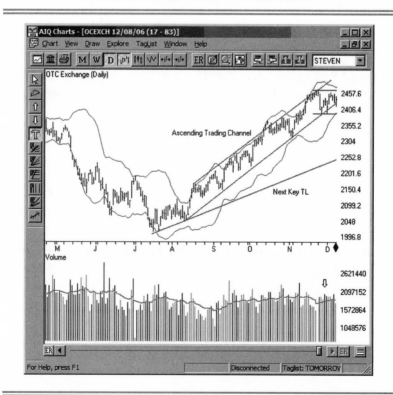

Courtesy of AIQ

12.10.06. The market pulled back to retest the lower boundary of the ascending trading channel again on Thursday and Friday. Thursday's distribution day was the third one in the last two weeks, which indicates more caution on the long side is warranted. Traders can become more cautious by reducing the number of positions they are trading or by reducing position sizes.

As long as the market remains within the current ascending trading channel, as shown on Figure 8.12, I will focus on trading longs. The distribution days during the last two weeks are an indication of some weakness in the market. The distribution days do not mean the market has to pullback, but they do increase the odds. Since the odds of a pullback have increased, I need to reduce my exposure a bit. If the market stops producing distribution days and starts showing accumulation, I will increase my exposure again.

If the market continues up without showing significant distribution, I will continue trading longs by replacing positions that hit their targets with new triggers. Since we have seen recent distribution, I will be looking for the stronger volume triggers and pass on ones that are below average volume. If the market continues showing distribution, I will keep reducing the number of positions I am willing to trade and look for stronger volume triggers.

New shorts are not yet attractive. The recent distribution is a warning sign, but as long as the market is trading within the ascending channel the trend is up and shorts carry above average risk. If the market clearly breaks below the lower boundary of the trading channel, I will add a couple of shorts and then look for a retest of the lower trend line from below and then a continuation down as a signal to increase the number of short positions beyond just a few. A break below the 2340 minor horizontal support area would also have me looking to increase the number of short positions.

If the market continues moving up within the ascending trading channel, I will take long triggers as my existing positions hit their targets. If the market moves to the upper ascending trend line, I will focus more on managing existing positions rather than adding new ones unless the market shows accumulation. If the market moves up on declining volume or continues to show distribution, I will reduce my number of long positions because moving up on declining volume is a warning sign.

In addition to the boundaries of the ascending trading channel, shown on Figure 8.12, I am watching the 2470 horizontal resistance area and the 2390 horizontal support area. A move above the horizontal resistance area on volume would mean I would slightly increase the number of positions. A move below the horizontal support level on volume would mean that I would increase the number of short positions from the first few initiated on a break below the lower boundary of the ascending trading channel.

EXAMPLE TRADING PLAN: UNUSUAL MARKET MOVES

When the market does something that seems unusual, backtesting techniques allow traders to find out how often it has happened and how the market has responded. Again, this approach allows traders to make fact-based decisions and not emotional ones. Figure 8.13 shows the market conditions on February 28, 2007, the day after the market showed the largest drop of the past couple of years.

My trading plan about the February 28 drop is summarized in the excerpt from *The Timely Trades Letter* of 02/02/07 below. As you read my market analysis, note that it describes the same techniques that I've outlined throughout this book. Ignore the talking heads on TV and analyze the price and volume patterns in the market.

> 02.02.07. The market showed a significant drop on huge volume during Tuesday's session. Our recent strategy of

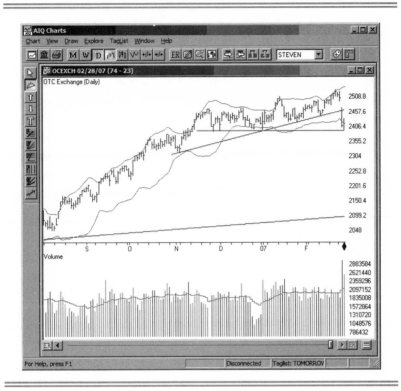

Courtesy of AIQ

caution, and not wanting to have a lot of money at risk, protected us from serious losses. As noted in recent Letters, the relatively flat period of the last few months and recent indecision implied weakness and caution. This is why I always want to see any market breakout prove itself by showing a successful retest, or continuation pattern, before significantly increasing exposure. Any run worth trading does not require you to be in the first few days, and getting in too early can hurt you.

Just a week ago the news was all about the DOW moving to multi-year highs, and how the markets were looking good. Now the same pundits are talking about a major correction. The DOW consists of just 30 huge cap stocks and is not representative of the overall market. It is more like a big cap

ETF than a market indicator. Successful traders watch the market itself, not what the pundits are saying.

The question is always, "what next," and the answer lies in market analysis. The NASDAQ has not seen a drop of over 90 points since 09/17/01 when the market fell 115 points. This type of move is unusual during recent years. However, the NASDAQ had 13 instances of 90 point or greater down days in 2001, with 36 of them in 2000.

The 49 days during 2000 and 2001 when the market was down, at least 90 points came during a very powerful bear market period. This was a great time to be short, or swing trading, and brutal if you were a buy and holder. The important question is; "what happened shortly after these drops," since that may shed some light on the current situation. I tested a strategy of buying the day after a 90 point or greater drop and holding for three days during the 2000 through 2001 period, when the market showed 49 of these strong one day drops. The interesting thing is that 51% of the trades were profitable and 49% of the trades were losing positions.

In the strongest bear market in recent memory (the period of 2000 to 2001), the odds of making money by buying the market the day after a 90 point or greater drop, and holding three days, were a coin flip. Even during a strong bear market, the plunges were followed by a *brief* bounce about half the time. When I ran the same test using a five day holding period, only 40% of the trades were profitable. With an eight day holding, 45% of the trades were profitable. Large down days lead to *short term bounces* about half the time.

This data indicates that a large drop is not strongly predictive in terms of the *short term direction*. This implies that we should continue to look at support and resistance levels, along with the Bollinger Bands, to determine the trading plan.

I also looked to see what some of the largest drops were in the period between the 115 point drop on 09/17/01 and today.

The only single day drop of 80 points or more during this period was Tuesday, 2/27/07. The only drop of 70 points or more was a 75 point drop on 10/17/01. There were four one day drops of 60 points or more with the most recent being a 64 point drop on 12/20/01.

The NASDAQ showed 22 single day drops of 50 points or more since 09/17/01 with the most recent being the 54 point drop on 11/27/06. The interesting thing about these recent large single day drops is that buying the morning after the large drop, and holding for three days, was profitable 72% of the time. Buying the day after the drop and holding for five days was profitable 65% of the time.

The strong bear market of 2000 and 2001 showed larger one day drops more often than the recent years, and yet the odds were about even that the market would be up three or four days later. The last six years have only shown four one day drops more than 60 points, and 22 more than 50 points. The interesting part is that in recent years the odds favored at least a small bounce after a large single day drop. This is why I will pick up a couple of longs if the market moves up in the next few days. I do not plan to hold them long, just in and out.

Does this data mean that the market *must* go up over the next few days? No, the odds favor it, but it is not a given. I do the research, know the odds, and trade when the odds are in my favor. This is why I will pick up a couple of longs if the market moves up in the next few days. I do not plan to hold them long, just in and out.

Nothing in the history of large one day drops implies that we should change the way trading plans are developed. Given this, let's review the market conditions and outline a trading plan for the rest of the week.

Tuesday's (2/27/07) huge volume move took the market below the short term ascending trend line, drawn between the lows of 11/03 and 01/03, which was our trigger to close any remaining open longs, and pick up a few shorts as outlined in the last Letter. We had three strong volume long triggers this week. FPL triggered Monday with well above average volume, then moved significantly above the upper Bollinger Band indicating it was time for a quick profit. AEP also triggered Monday on strong volume, but it did not hit a target, and it reversed during Tuesday's market drop for a small loss. DPL triggered on Monday with strong volume and did not quite hit the upper Band. It reversed during Tuesday's action for a small loss.

When the market broke the short term ascending trend line on Tuesday, I followed the plan by closing any remaining longs and looking for a few shorts. Given the huge down volume on the NASDAQ, I shorted the QQQQ. In addition to trading the Q's, recent short setups from the Letter that triggered on volume include BMC, LXK, and QLGC. BMC hit the lower Bollinger Band after triggering for a nice 4 ½% profit. LXK triggered on strong volume and moved below the lower Band for a quick 4% profit.

Tuesday's action moved the market well below the lower Bollinger Band, which is a condition that rarely lasts long. During today's action, the market tested horizontal support in the 2390 area then bounced up on strong volume and retested the lower Bollinger Band. At this point the market has three choices: continue down, bounce, or move sideways in a narrow range.

If the market decides to move down immediately, I will be cautious since it closed today right on the lower Bollinger Band. Adding new shorts when the market is near the lower Bollinger Band carries above average risk. I would like to see a little more bounce or some sideways movement to let the market pull away from the Band before getting serious about picking up short positions.

For traders that are unable to take short positions in certain accounts, take a look at DOG, PSQ, and SH, which are ETFs that are inversely correlated to the DOW, QQQQ, and SPY. Taking positions in these ETFs may allow one to profit from declines in the respective index.

If the market moves sideways a couple of days, or bounces a bit then continues down, I will watch for a break below horizontal support in the 2390 area as a signal to add a few more strong volume shorts. Just as I wanted to see any potential move up prove itself before getting aggressive, I now want to see any move down prove itself by a successful retest of support or a successful continuation pattern before significantly increasing the number of trading positions. On any initial move below horizontal support, I will be looking at trading a few short positions. I will then increase the number of positions and the position sizes if and when the move proves itself.

If the market decides to bounce from current levels, I will look for a move above the 2430 area on above average volume as a signal to pick up a few long positions. I would continue to focus on triggers with above average volume and take profits quickly after about 3% or three days. The interesting thing about longs on a bounce is that there is a huge gap on the daily from Tuesday's action, and these gaps often close within a week or ten days. Just to stay on the safe side, I would look at taking profits on longs as the market approaches the short term ascending trend line drawn between the lows of 11/03 and 01/03.

Writing down your analysis of the market and developing a trading plan every evening helps you understand what is normal in the market and how to react to times when the market does something unusual. In general, the way to trade is to position to profit if the market does the usual thing, such as bouncing off support or retracing from resistance. When the market does something unusual, it is best to exercise caution and reduce risk.

MARKET ADAPTIVE TRADING SUMMARY

A summary of the techniques I use in market adaptive trading:

- Understand market statistics so you know if current conditions are favorable or high risk.

- Develop multiple trading systems and carefully test them in all three types of market conditions.

- Use trend lines to help determine the current market conditions and select the appropriate trading tools.

- When the market breaks a trend line, become cautious. Reduce holding times, position sizes, and number of trading positions until the next move is clear.

- Avoid trading when the market is in a narrow basing area.

- Have a clear idea of where NASDAQ support and resistance are and concentrate trades around these areas.

The market will not adapt to us, so we must adapt to it. The way to get started in market adaptive trading is to use backtesting and experience to develop knowledge about how the market usually behaves in a given situation. Additional information on this may be found at www.daisydogger.com. Based on this knowledge, traders can position themselves to profit if the market does the usual thing, which by definition it does most of the time. Remember to plan the trades, and trade the plan.

STEVE PALMQUIST is a trader with more than 20 years of market experience who puts his own money to work in the market every day. Steve has shared trading techniques and systems at seminars across the country, presented at the Traders Expo, and published trading articles in *Stocks & Commodities, Traders Journal, The Opening Bell,* and *Working Money.* Steve is the founder of www.daisydogger.com, which provides trading tips and techniques, and the publisher of *The Timely Trades Letter,* in which he shares his market analysis, trading setups, and trading tips twice a week. Steve holds a BSEE from Washington State University, and a Masters in Electrical Engineering from the University of Illinois. Steve has been involved in the management and development of communications systems, high speed computers, test equipment, infrared vision systems, and color printers at companies such as Bell Laboratories, Integrated Measurement Systems, Flir Systems, and Tektronix. He holds 10 U.S. patents. Steve is a father of four, and has a private pilot license with an instrument rating.

INDEX

definitions

    bearish engulfing patterns, 64–66, 88

    bullish engulfing patterns, 28, 60–61

    clarifying, 32, 94, 143–44

    downtrend, 54, 205–6

    evening star patterns, 160, 161–63, 169, 174–84, 191

    hammer patterns, 89, 104–5, 112

    hanging man patterns, 113, 134

    morning star patterns, 137–38, 156–57

    uptrend market, 57, 203

DIA (Diamonds Trust, Series 1), 159, 160

distribution days, 211–12

DO (Diamond Offshore Drl), 65, 66

dollar value filters. See stock price filters

Dow-Jones Industrial Average (DJIA), 213–14

downtrend filters

    bearish engulfing patterns, 69–70, 72–73, 83–88

    bullish engulfing patterns, 45

    hanging man pattern, 119–22

downtrend market

    definition of, 54, 205–6

    NASDAQ, 69–70, 83–84, 85, 119–22

    and trend line breaks, 203

DPHIQ (Delphi Corp.), 114, 115

DPL (DPL Inc.), 216

drawdowns, 23–24, 102

LXK (Lexmark Intl. Inc.), 216

R

S

TRADING
RESOURCE
GUIDE

RECOMMENDED READING

21 CANDLESTICKS EVERY TRADER SHOULD KNOW

by Melvin Pasternak

Why do candlesticks continue to gain power in the market? The answer can be found in the clear and straight-forward nature of the candlesticks themselves—they allow you to see the bigger picture. Continuation patterns, reversal patterns, emerging trends, bottom and tops—all other charting systems can't compete with the insightful power of candles. Out of hundreds of charts, Dr. Pasternak discovered 21 candlesticks every trader must know, and he's ready to share them with you.

Item #BCSPx4050479 • List Price: $19.95

STRATEGIES FOR PROFITING WITH JAPANESE CANDLESTICK CHARTS

by Steve Nison

What are Japanese Candlesticks—and why should traders use them? This DVD workshop helps you understand and master this powerful tool with high impact results. Steve Nison is the world's foremost expert on Candlesticks—and now you can benefit from his expertise in the comfort of your own home. Filmed at a unique one-day seminar he gave for a select group of traders, it's an incredible opportunity to have the foremost expert guide you to trading success.

Item #BCSPx2434165 • List Price: $695.00

THE CANDLESTICK COURSE

by Steve Nison

In this coursebook, Steve Nison explains patterns of varying complexity and tests the reader's knowledge with quizzes, Q&As, and intensive examples. In accessible and easy-to-understand language, this book offers expert instruction on the practical applications of candlestick charting. Straightforward answers quickly clarify this profitable charting method. This guide will allow you to recognize and implement various candlestick patterns and lines in a real-world trading environment—giving you a noticeable edge over other traders.

Item #BCSPx84668 • List Price: $70.00

PROVEN CANDLESTICK PATTERNS

by Steve Palmquist

Candles are an effective tool for extracting profits from the market. But there are hundreds of candles, and thousands of strategies for you to consider. How do you know which ones will work for you?

This 90-minute course arms you with what you need to know about candlestick patterns. It shows you the candlesticks you should be using and which ones you should avoid. Most traders spend years collecting this powerful information, and you'll have access to it all at once! Don't let another day go by without knowing these proven candlestick patterns!

Item #BCSPx5197576 • List Price: $99.00

MARKET WIZARDS

by Jack D. Schwager

How do the world's most successful traders make millions of dollars in a year... or sometimes in just hours? Are they masters of a priceless wizardry or simply the very lucky winners in a random market lottery that allows only a few players to become fantastically wealthy? What are the secrets of their unheard-of success? Market expert Jack D. Schwager interviews top traders in a variety of markets and determines that an interesting mix of method and mental posture is largely responsible. Market Wizards takes you inside the minds of these most remarkable traders. Understand what it takes to succeed, and hear it in the words of the Market Wizards themselves.

Item #BCSPx4050480 • List Price: $17.95

▲ ▲ ▲ ▲ ▲ ▲

To get the current lowest price on any item listed
Go to www.traderslibrary.com

Free 2 Week Trial Offer for U.S. Residents From Investor's Business Daily:

I NVESTOR'S BUSINESS DAILY will provide you with the facts, figures, and objective news analysis you need to succeed.

Investor's Business Daily is formatted for a quick and concise read to help you make informed and profitable decisions.

To take advantage of this free 2 week trial offer, e-mail us at customerservice@fpbooks.com or visit our website at www.fpbooks.com where you find other free offers as well.

You can also reach us by calling 1-800-272-2855 or fax us at 410-964-0027.